Choosing for Cruising

Also by Bruce Roberts-Goodson:

Spray: The Ultimate Cruising Boat
ISBN 0-7136-4086-3

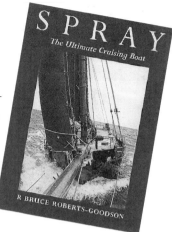

Spray was the first boat ever to be sailed single-handed around the world over 100 years ago. This famous voyage, was one of the major feats of single-handed sailing of all time. Rebuilt extensively, this 36 foot vessel travelled 46,000 miles in three years, without any of the modern equipment that today's sailors take for granted.

The book explores the rebuilding of *Spray*, analyses her design, lines plans and sail plan, gives highlights of the record-setting voyage, and recounts the building, sailing and cruising experiences of owners of over 800 *Spray* replicas and copies which have since been built.

Other titles of interest:

How to Choose the Right Yacht
Joachim F Muhs
ISBN 0-7136-3950-4
This book shows how interested buyers can assess whether a boat is fast or slow, wet or dry, holds its course well, is light on the helm, rides the waves comfortably, will respond to a light breeze and whether it can be sailed easily by a small family crew – and all this from the comfort of one's own home!

Living Afloat
Clare Allcard
ISBN 0-7136-4135-5
Whether crew, skipper or mate, and whether stepping aboard for a week, a year or a lifetime, *Living Afloat* makes the perfect companion to adventure. No matter what the problem is, from storing up, educating children afloat, coping with sunburn or malaria, to disposing of rubbish, fixing the heads or washing clothes in the minimum of fresh water – it is all here.

Choosing for Cruising

How to select and equip the perfect
cruising yacht

Bruce Roberts-Goodson

Adlard Coles Nautical
London

Published by Adlard Coles Nautical 1998
an imprint of A & C Black (Publishers) Ltd
35 Bedford Row, London WClR 4JH

ISBN 0-7136-4416-8

A CIP catalogue record for this book is available from the British Library.

Typeset in Galliard 10.5/13 by Penny Mills
Printed and bound in Great Britain by Hillman Printers (Frome) Ltd

Contents

Acknowledgements

So many people have contributed to the information in this book that it is impossible to name but a few. One of my first research projects was to review the hundreds of letters received from owners of cruising boats who were *'out there doing it'*. In addition are those sailors who have approached me at many boat shows and offered comments, advice and suggestions. These people were always willing to tell what helped to make their cruising successful and what could be done to improve their safety and enjoyment.

Very special thanks are due to the following people: to my wife Gwenda, who has supported me in my work for over thirty years; she has not hesitated to impose the women's view when it came to designing items in which she was particularly interested. As a very active first mate, these items were not restricted to the galley and other stereotype areas of the design. My thanks to Andrew Slorach, my long time partner and associate who has been my severest critic and is always ready to offer constructive advice; to George Love, my boat building mentor; Philip Sheaf my UK agent, and finally to all those in the boating industry who, over the past 30 years, have helped me to chart a course through the shoals that have claimed so many who have tried to turn their hobby into a business; to all of you my sincere thanks.

Introduction

First a little history. In my opinion, cruising as we understand it today – meaning long distance sailing in small boats for pleasure rather than for profit – began in the late 1890's. It all started when retired sea captain Joshua Slocum found that he could not make a living out of the rebuilt former oyster dragger, the 36 ft 9 in (11.2 m) *Spray*. The record of Slocum's rebuilding the *Spray* and his subsequent adventures have inspired tens of thousands of cruising people to cruise in their own boats ever since he wrote *Sailing Alone Around the World*.

In Slocum's wake have come many thousands of cruising sailors, some of whom have become well-known personalities as a result of their exploits. One not so well known early cruising sailor was Fred Rebel. Fred not only made history in 1931 when he sailed from Australia to USA in an 18 ft (5.5 m) skiff, he also made his own charts! Indeed, not only his own charts but every item of navigational equipment and put them to the test over 9000 miles of ocean.

Fred Rebel was a carpenter down on his luck and had fled his native Latvia in the wake of revolution to arrive in Australia just in time for the start of the Great Depression. After a series of successes and failures in his new country and the sight of thousands of his host countrymen clearing out to the bush, Fred decided to move on towards California. So, with no job and little over £100 capital, Fred began the second migration of his life, this time by small boat.

He bought one of the well-known Sydney Harbour 18-footers, a very fast boat with an inordinate spread of canvas. It had, in fact, so large a sail plan that in anything much more than a zephyr it needed a burly crew of 16 to keep it upright. It has been accurately described as the most spectacular racing boat in the world, and the very worst to sail across an ocean. However, this was the boat Fred chose and he immediately set about strengthening her and fitting a canvas spray cover as a crude cabin.

Work on the boat was straightforward, he was a carpenter and he knew about wood. Navigational preparations on the other hand were an immense challenge, particularly to a man whose sea experience had been limited to a steamer's stoke-hold. He spent his days pouring over books in the public library until finally he acquired a 70 year old navigation manual. The library's atlas from which he compiled his charts must have been of an even earlier vintage, about the time of Cook's last voyage by the sound of it, for when Fred later came to use his charts he found quite important groups of islands missed out entirely. But his most interesting achievement was in the construction of his navigational instruments which he describes as follows:

The materials I used for my sextant were several pieces of hoop-iron; a Boy Scout telescope, price one shilling; an old hacksaw blade; and a stainless steel table knife. I broke pieces off the table knife to make the mirrors. They had to be ground optically flat, which I accomplished by melting a lump of bitumen on to them for finger-grips and by rubbing them over emery-cloth laid on a piece of plate glass. I used three grades of emery cloth—coarse, medium and fine and finally I gave the steel a mirror finish by rubbing it on a damp cloth with red oxide (or jeweller's rouge).

The hacksaw blade was for the degree scale. I chose it because of its regularly cut teeth and because I could bend it into an arc. I also chose the radius of arc so that two teeth made one degree. I took the temper out of the blade so that I should be able to reshape the teeth, and for a tangent screw I took an ordinary wood screw, that would engage nicely with the hacksaw. This way I could read half-degrees of arc straight off the teeth of the hacksaw. But half a degree of latitude represents 30 nautical miles and you need far greater accuracy than that. So I enlarged the head of the screw, and subdivided its circumference by sixty. Thus I was able to read to minutes of the arc off the screw head itself, that was the hardest job to make.

A chronometer was essential. Fred could not make one so he did the next best thing and bought two cheap watches (each as a check on the other) for a few shillings. He wrote 'I slung them in gimbals, so that the motion of the boat could not affect them.'

Another essential instrument handmade was the taffrail-log. He wrote, 'I made my spinner from a bit of broomstick, to which I set aluminium blades at such an angle that the spinner would turn once for every 12 in of passage through the water. For the indicator I adapted a little clock, gearing it down so that every minute on its face should mean one mile of distance sailed. When I tried this log out, I found there was a slip of 20 per cent; but an error in a nautical instrument does not matter, provided it is constant, you can allow for it. And until the time when the works of the little clock corroded with the sea air and water, this taffrail-log served me well.'

Fred left Sydney in his boat *Elaine* on 31 December 1931 and arrived in America one year and three days later.

This narrative is not intended as an invitation for you to rush out and start looking for the perfect 18 ft (5.5 m) cruising boat. The experiences of Fred Rebel are included to illustrate just how small some boats are that people have acquired when choosing for cruising. For more information on those who have gone before see recommended reading in Appendix 2.

You do not have to intend to set off around the world when you make the decision to adopt the cruising lifestyle. Weekend sailors can enjoy their cruising just as much as long distance sailors. As with all endeavours there seems to be a perceived (in my experience often erroneous) pecking order among cruising folk. Do not try to emulate the singlehanded, three times around the world person, if that is not your thing. Cruising can be enjoyed

close to home equally well. You can adopt the sensible attitude and gradually extend your cruising grounds as your experience and other circumstances permit. What has this to do with *choosing for cruising*? In my opinion it is a big factor. So many people's cruising plans have come to grief because they felt obliged to overstate and then overreach *their own* sensible cruising goals.

French Canadians Claude and Genevieve Desjardins have sailed nearly half way round the world in this diminutive 18-footer.

Cruising will mean different things to different people; your cruising may be coastal in nature and all undertaken within 100 miles (or less) of your home port. You may prefer gunkholing either locally or in some nearby cruising ground. If, on the other hand you are going to make that world-girdling voyage, then you will need to give even more serious consideration to selecting the right boat. Of course many successful voyages have been accomplished in unsuitable boats, but here we are trying to avoid depending on large slices of luck.

Choosing just where you intend to cruise may be one of the hardest decisions you will have to make. Being honest with oneself will play an important part in this decision. It is always more romantic to dream of far off locations than it is to admit to yourself (and friends) that what you would really like to enjoy is some local cruising involving minimum hassle and maximum relaxation.

Where you intend to cruise will definitely influence your choice of boat. As you read each chapter you will be able to relate various types of hull configuration, keel types, accommodation layouts etc., to a particular type of usage. Some boats are suitable for sailing in many and varied locations, while others are more specialised. This book will try to guide you through these areas of choice.

During 30 years as a naval architect, I have always tried to design boats where safety was of paramount importance and this brings us to the subject of multihulls. In the early 1960's I was associated with the late Hedley Nicol who at that time was a multihull designer of some note. My function was to manage our mutually owned boat yard and kit business. Eventually Hedley confided in me that he was becoming disillusioned with trimarans and indeed multihulls in general, believing that the possibility of capsize offset many of the advantages that we had all enjoyed when sailing multi's.

It is hard to imagine that in 1961 there had been very few cruising multihull capsizes; in fact there were few cruising multihulls in existence. Of course all that was to change dramatically in the mid and late 1960's right through to the present day, when multihull capsizes are relatively common.

Subsequently, Hedley and many other trimaran enthusiasts lost their lives in trimaran disasters; mostly capsizes and the occasional loss from structural failure. Catamarans while also being prone to capsize under difficult wind and sea conditions, do have a marginally better safety record than trimarans. Contrary to popular belief, multihulls can sink (see the article *The Sinking of Catrena* by Brian Coe, *Practical Boat Owner* December 1995).

The fact that multihulls make *comparatively* few ocean crossings, convinces me that it is not only the anti-multihull fraternity that are concerned about the possibility of a capsize in mid ocean. If you totally disagree with me about the safety of multihulls, please gather all the information you can, read everything available, and then make your own decision.

A book of this type enters treacherous waters and I do not suggest you follow the advice blindly. Cruising people are often very opinionated; in some ways this is what gives them the confidence which in time combined with experience, makes their cruising successful. As soon as you mention to anyone remotely connected with the sea that you are planning a cruise in your own boat you will receive a plethora of advice. In the following pages I have tried to sort out not only the type of advice you should consider but also to alert you to the questions, to which you will need answers.

Without previous experience, would-be cruising folk can sometimes be led to, at best, choosing an unsatisfactory boat, or at worst creating the conditions that lead to a disaster that will put paid to their cruising ambitions forever. Some of you may have met individuals who have tried cruising and failed; all that follows is my attempt to guide you and your family to a successful cruising experience that will last as long as you all find it rewarding and enjoyable.

This happy couple, Herbert and Petra Fritz, built their Roberts 53 steel sailboat themselves. Herbert spent 5 years full time on the project and literally made everything himself. Some of the fittings that Herbert made are featured in later chapters.

Herbert and Petra have just completed a succesful three year circumnavigation.

You will notice the frequent mention of the word *family* throughout the text; family can mean wife, partner, children and perhaps even one or more pets. If you do not consider the family from the very beginning then your cruising experience will be short-lived. The most common story related by those who have tried cruising and failed, is one where it was assumed that the entire family would share and enjoy the type of cruising you have in mind. This attitude leads to frequent arguments, or worse; sometimes desertions and separations at the first port of call.

As mentioned earlier, cruising people are often opinionated and as such will often recommend or decry a specific product, being more than happy to make sure you note the brand name. I too have often recommended products or services by name, but be warned; in this changing world where takeovers of companies are commonplace, the quality of products often changes for better or worse. Make your own investigations, read all the product comparisons and reports, above all become well informed.

CHAPTER 1

Budgets and Planning

◆ *Cruise planning and calculations of how much will it all cost* ◆ *How to save money and keep within your budget* ◆ *Budgets for acquiring your boat and for maintaining the cruising lifestyle* ◆ *VAT certificates* ◆ *The KISS factor* ◆ *Earn as you cruise* ◆ *Your boat may play a part in your income* ◆ *Chartering your boat* ◆ *Boat size for cruising and crew requirements* ◆ *Where to look: new or secondhand or build your own?*

When you are just starting to explore the possibilities of your (first or next) cruising boat, budgeting is a depressing subject. Unfortunately the subject of finance will be one of the foremost things you will need to consider. Everything to do with cruising has a price and some form of budget is required at every step from your first planning session onwards. If you do not have a well planned budget, you are unlikely to have a successful cruise.

DEFINE YOUR CRUISING GOALS

What type of cruising do you have in mind? Occasional weekends and annual holidays? Long-term or full-time cruising? The answer to these questions will have a great bearing on your budget requirements. If you are planning the former, your biggest expense will be the boat itself, whereas if you are considering long-term voyaging your budget considerations will become more complex.

Once you have clearly defined your cruising objectives then your budget can take shape. The last thing you will want is to end up with a mountain of debt when you return. All cruising experiences have a beginning (planning), middle (the cruise which may last for a number of years) and an end (the day you sell your boat and take on a shore-based existence).

Cruising from the UK and Europe

Cruising full time could involve leaving the UK in September and utilising the trade wind route to make the West Indies for Christmas; cruising in that area until spring and then returning to the UK, taking about 12 months to accomplish the round trip. Thousands of cruising boats make this type of voyage each year including those who make detours to encompass the Atlantic islands and the Mediterranean. Heading into the Pacific takes a bigger commitment, one that you may wish to consider after you have explored areas nearer to home.

Cruising from the USA

Sailing boats based on the US east coast often restrict their cruising to their own scenic coastline, heading to Maine or down to Florida and the east coast of Mexico, or out to the various islands of the Caribbean. For these sailors, crossing the Atlantic is the big commitment. US west coast sailors usually cruise up to the San Juan Islands off Washington State and the Canadian Gulf islands and then possibly on to Alaska. Other west coast boats head for Mexico and are faced with the big decision whether to head out into the Pacific. West coast sailors have the option of an exploratory cruise to Hawaii; if they find long sea passages are not for them then they can simply return to the west coast and the thousands of miles of beautiful cruising.

Cruising from Australia

Australian yachtsmen also have many choices; with their huge coastline, and the proximity of the Pacific islands, they have plenty of places to explore before taking off on a long cruise. East coast sailors often head for Lord Howe Island and use this round trip as their shake-down cruise.

Cruising from a foreign port

Those committed to long-distance and full-time cruising, who are considering the options given above, may prefer to travel by conventional means to their chosen cruising location. You can acquire your boat in the area where you want to commence cruising. At many of these locations you will find boats for sale belonging to people who have not planned their cruise as well as you have! For example if you live in the UK and you have in mind some Pacific cruising, you will find the market for used boats in Australia very advantageous. The prices in Australian dollars, when converted into sterling, make the boats seem very inexpensive.

The same applies to UK residents with their eyes on the Caribbean; there is a good selection of used boats to be had in the USA especially in Florida. Other good places to look for a suitable boat are those areas which are the first major port of call for cruising boats. These include Hawaii, Noumea, Fiji and the Azores, as well as places in and around the Mediterranean such as Gibraltar, Portugal, Spain, Greece and Turkey, where you can often find a bargain. Exchange rates fluctuate and the currency exchange rates may well determine whether to purchase locally or abroad.

Visitors to Europe

For those US, Australian, New Zealand and other non-European residents who want to cruise the Mediterranean, and perhaps cruise through the French, Dutch and Belgian Canals (highly recommended), the idea of obtaining a boat in Europe has its attractions. For one thing the long ocean crossing can be avoided. There is also the possibility of having the boat built in the countries of the former Eastern bloc where labour costs are low. The very reasonable building and labour costs of the UK (compared with Germany and certain other EU countries) make acquiring a suitable boat in this country worth serious consideration.

The recently enacted European Recreational Craft Directive (RCD) and the requirement to pay VAT on boats remaining in EU waters for over six months, make it a sensible alternative for non-EU residents to buy their boat within the EU. Non-EU residents who bring their boats into EU waters will need to pay the VAT or limit their stay to less than six months. The current rate varies between 15 per cent and 20 per cent depending in which EU country you are located when the tax is due and payable.

Cost saving is not the only reason (although it can be a very good one) for buying your boat abroad. In some cases time restrictions, unwillingness of your partner to undertake long ocean crossings, and numerous other circumstances may make the idea of starting from a distant port an attractive option.

After cruising?

You should budget for all aspects of your future lifestyle. Most people tend to ignore the last part of the exercise; they either think they will never return to a shore-based life, or they just ignore the subject altogether. You can plan and budget for all main stages of your cruising adventure including the end, and still not detract from the overall excitement. A well chosen boat capable of holding or enhancing its value, will help to provide you with a re-establishment fund if you move ashore. This is not to suggest that you necessarily put a limit on the length of your cruising experience; many cruising individuals, partners and couples like Eric and Susan Hiscock, enjoy a cruising lifestyle for many years. You should be aware that some time in the distant future, you may need to re-establish yourself ashore. Each individual or couple will have limits of one form or another. Lifetime partnerships often start when couples meet in foreign ports, children are born, and other factors may require a change to your plans.

APPORTIONING AVAILABLE FUNDS

Now to get down to specifics. Let us assume you have a certain amount of money available and you have caught the cruising bug. As yet you do not have a vessel or perhaps the boat you currently own is unsuitable for the type of cruising you have in mind. The first sizeable chunk of your budget will be for the acquisition of the boat. You will have several options includ-

Honeymead moored off Morea. Chester and Norma Lemon built this 44 ft (13.4m) boat and cruised from Australia, to Alaska, West coast USA, Mexico, Line Islands, Japan and China covering over 75,000 miles before trading their boat for a piece of a tropical island in the Coral sea.

ing having a boat designed and built to your requirements, building your own from a suitable design, buying new, or finding a suitable second-hand craft. It would be difficult to set an accurate budget until you have investigated each of these options.

The second main budgetary consideration for those who plan either to cruise full time or continuously for several months each year, will be the expenses associated with day-to-day living, items such as food and clothing, boat maintenance, mooring and haul out fees. Add to this, visas and other associated paperwork, which can often be more expensive than expected. There will be the cost of additional gear and equipment such as replacement of lost or worn out items, plus new charts, pilot books and the like.

It is a wise cruising person who first spends time covering many sheets of paper with figures. After you have arrived at what looks like a workable budget, you can start to look for a suitable boat to be your cruising home for the weeks, months or perhaps even years ahead.

The VAT factor

You will need to explore the VAT minefield. From 1 January 1993, when the EU single fiscal area came into being, boats could be transferred and sold freely between residents of EU countries without duty being levied, provided that evidence was produced that VAT had been paid on the particular vessel.

This radius chine steel 44 ft (13.4 m) sailing boat *Baltic Rose* was built in Riga Latvia by a professional yard for a Swedish client.

The best proof of VAT-paid status is the 'green flimsy': the EU standard document that is issued when VAT is paid on a new boat. For older boats where VAT was paid before the VAT rules were properly documented, the next best thing is an original letter from the Customs office stating that in their opinion they are satisfied that VAT has been paid on the vessel. In the UK you should contact your local HM Customs office, where you can obtain up-to-date information on what is required for you to formalise the VAT-paid status on your present vessel or a boat you are interested in purchasing.

A special exemption exists on boats built before January 1985; if a boat was in European waters on 31 December 1992 and the owner can prove it, then it is VAT exempt. If the boat was built *after* this then VAT will sooner or later have to be or will already have been paid. Where the boat was located on 31 December 1992 is the deciding factor as to where VAT has to be paid. In my own case the UK built *K*I*S*S* was in Holland on the fateful date and that is where the VAT was paid before I consented to purchase the boat. My current boat was built in Holland in 1991 but was in the UK on the 31 December 1992 so the VAT was paid in the UK. As the green flimsy did not exist for this boat it was necessary for the seller to obtain a letter from the UK Customs stating that they accepted the proffered evidence that the VAT was paid. This original letter along with previous owners' bills of sale, builders' invoices and SSR certificate now forms part of the ship's papers.

There is a quirk in the VAT laws: the rule being that if you purchase a VAT-paid boat outside the EU and then bring it back into EU waters then you will have to pay the VAT. If you are considering buying a VAT-paid boat that is currently located outside EU waters, make sure it is returned to an EU country and check the VAT status before you make the purchase.

Additional equipment

Even the best equipped boat will require many additional items to meet your particular needs. My own Spray 28 *K*I*S*S* was 'well found' when I acquired her. She had been built by an American couple Hal and Dorothy

Stufft and equipped for the kind of cruising that I had in mind, at least for the following two or three seasons. The last two years' expenses for her show that the equipment I subsequently added totalled some thousands of pounds. She did come *well* equipped but obviously not *totally* equipped so extra funds must be put aside for unexpected expenses including taxes and additional items of equipment that you may have overlooked but will require for one reason or another.

This brings us to the KISS factor, the initials being an acronym for 'keep it simple sailor' or less politely 'keep it simple stupid'. This saying, which I am told originated in the engineering industry, it is well worth remembering when considering all things boating.

Budget for the best

When budgeting for additional items to complete the fitting out of your cruising boat, always consider buying the best. Perhaps that will be the best you can afford, but nevertheless this should be the best. Most experienced cruising people can relate stories of their own regrets at cutting corners, when purchasing boating gear. Naturally you will be looking for the best price, but if you allow a known price for a particular item and are then able to obtain it at a better price, you will be able to offset the cost overruns that will certainly occur.

Boat jumbles

In my opinion one of the greatest British marine institutions is the 'boat jumble'. This wonderful source of inexpensive, often top quality equipment and boating gear, is unparalleled in most other countries. After attending the Beaulieu Jumble, the grand-daddy of all boating jumbles, I was sold on the idea. Unless you have considerable boating experience, you should attend these jumbles accompanied by a knowledgeable boating friend. Know what you are looking for and only part with your money if you are absolutely sure of the suitability of the item for your boat. Make sure you are confident of the quality and you should have checked the best prices available from more conventional sources. Assure yourself that the item was legally obtained by the vendor! When it comes to price, haggle like your life depended on it. Under no circumstances buy something 'that you think may come in handy', but for which you have no specific need; most boat owners' homes and boats have a collection of such items; the smart ones sell them at the next available jumble.

CRUISING INCOME

So far we have only discussed the budgetary outgoings. Those of you who are planning to retire or take an extended break from your normal employment should consider how you can generate some income as you cruise. If you are planning weekend and annual holiday cruises, then you will most likely have a regular income and this may not apply to you.

Apart from leasing your house while you are away, one of the more obvious earners is chartering. Although this is so obvious as to be over-worked when it comes to expectations, it is surprising just how many cruising people make a success of *part-time* charter. If you have the right boat and perhaps just as importantly, the right disposition to deal with charter parties or individuals, this is worth your consideration. *Part-time* charter can mean a couple of weeks per year for some expense-sharing friends or several short charters by strangers who come recommended to you in one way or another. Unless you are running a full-time professional charter operation, you should choose carefully when deciding who will spend time as a paying guest aboard your boat.

Consider you and your partner's personal skills. The obvious ones include boatbuilding experience in any material. You may have obtained your boatbuilding experience by building and/or fitting out your own boat. This is a factor worth considering when you are deciding how you will acquire your boat. The actual building and fitting out of a reasonable sized cruising boat will certainly add to your marketable skills.

Most tradespeople have marketable skills, welders, metal workers, car-penters, plumbers and electricians will find part-time employment not only ashore but among their less handy cruising contemporaries. If you have some experience with the maintenance and repair of electronic equipment you will be *very* much in demand.

Dentists, doctors, chiropractors and other professionals can often earn worthwhile fees both ashore and among the cruising population. Some licensing requirements may interfere with your activities ashore but it is worth investigating in advance where you can legally practise. You may be able to obtain a licence in those areas you plan to visit. Language skills can be turned into cash as can secretarial experience. Computer literacy is a definite skill and one that will always find a ready market. Writing articles and perhaps a book on your experiences is another possibility; be aware that there is a limited market for these latter skills and they are not very well paid.

Adapting your boat to generate income

The planning stage is when you should decide if the boat itself will play a part in earning income as you cruise. The prospect of chartering may cause you to select a certain type of layout to allow some separation between the hosts and guests. If you are planning to earn income from a trade or pro-fession then you may wish to include a workshop or work space in the accommodation layout. You will have your own ideas of how important the work space is to your future cruising needs. Do not become carried away with this element; you will be better advised to make the work area fit the boat rather than choose the boat to fit the work area!

This 53 ft steel boat *Akvavit* was purpose built by professional fisherman, Harrison Smith, to be used as a sailing fishboat and as a family cruiser. After several years of cruising and successful commercial fishing, she has proved her worth in every respect.

WHAT SIZE SHOULD THE BOAT BE?

Over the years my office has dealt with hundreds of thousands of enquiries from those who intend taking up the cruising lifestyle. One of the most asked questions is 'how big a boat should I choose?' Our reply is always the same, '*choose the smallest boat that will satisfy your current requirements*'. Will your children want to accompany you when they are past the early teenage years? Do not expect to have a continual stream of friends and relatives who are clamouring to join you for various sections of your voyage. Unless you are very wealthy, do not choose a size of boat that will require a crew to handle the vessel. As for the upper size range; well set up cruising sailing boats up to 55 ft (16.75 m) can be handled by a two-person crew; this includes a husband and wife combination. How small is too small? One Canadian couple built and sailed a Roberts-designed 18 ft (5.48 m) trailer sailer from Montreal to Australia; they even took their cat along. Please do not take this latter example as a recommendation.

Size is not everything, however: you may decide to start with the largest hull that your budget allows. The main thing, is to not overextend your budget. You cannot assume that your children or friends will want to cruise with you on a long term basis. Unless you plan to charter, do not allow the 'guest cabin or spare berths' to dictate your choice of size of hull or interior arrangement.

Gunkholing

When I think of gunkholing it brings to mind lazy sailing and exploring in protected bays and estuaries and rivers. For this type of sailing your

Designed as a trailer sailer, several boats of this design have made extensive offshore passages.

cruising boat can be as small as you wish; a considerable amount of this type of activity is undertaken in open boats. When it is time to anchor at night, a boom cover often serves as a shelter. Portable gas or primus stove and a bucket may be all the 'appliances' carried on this cruising boat.

The right boat and an inquisitive mind are two important qualifications for this type of cruising. Shallow draft is a major benefit. Once the water gets really shallow you will no longer be able to rely on your depth sounder so you will have to feel your way in many of these areas. Detailed charts of the area you are exploring are essential, if none are available then it may be fun to make your own, thus enhancing the enjoyment of the current trip plus adding to the enjoyment of future visitors to the area.

Nature watching is one of the many attractions of gunkholes. You may also find oddities: follies, abandoned fishing and other commercial operations, historical relics and occasionally a human eccentric. I can claim to have encountered them all and on reflection they bring back pleasant memories.

Trailer sailing

The size of your trailer sailer will be restricted by the width limits placed on road vehicles by the authorities in various countries or individual states. In general, the width limit is 8 ft (2.43 m); however, in some places it is a little more generous but usually never exceeding 9 ft (2.74 m) without special permits. As far as the length is concerned, a boat with 8 ft (2.43 m) beam should not exceed 28 ft (8.53 m) in overall length. Before you restrict yourself to the local legal trailer width, you may want to consider just how often you really intend to move the boat by road. Many people find it is easier to leave their trailer sailer in the water all season and just bring it

This fibreglass Spray 22 is ideal for trailing to desirable cruising locations.

home for winter storage; if this is your situation then it may be more useful to exceed the trailerable width limit by owning a 'pocket cruiser' and obtain a permit to move the boat to and from the water twice a year.

If you intend to use your boat as a true cruising trailer sailer then you will need to check width limits and other requirements for the areas where you operate the boat. In the EU (European Union) these regulations are being harmonised. This agreement will make trailer sailing much more attractive; you can take your boat from the UK by ferry and trail it anywhere in Europe (using it as a camper or caravan along the way) and commence your cruising from some desirable location. You could even leave your boat and trailer safely tucked up in a boatyard ready for the following season. If you cannot afford a large boat or if you prefer some of the benefits of owning a smaller vessel, including lower initial investment and less maintenance, then a trailer sailer or pocket cruiser may suit you best.

BUY OR BUILD?

In this area your choices lie between buying new, having a boat custom built, purchasing second hand or building from a hull and deck package or perhaps from plans and patterns. These choices are all affected by your particular requirements. You and your partner's present age, financial situation, family considerations and perhaps the desire to get on with it, can influence your choice in this matter. Many people approaching retirement plan well ahead and have all the above options available. Those with foresight can have the boat ready for their retirement and enjoy uninterrupted cruising.

Buying new

Buying new is an obvious option. If you buy a new stock boat, you will find that it will most likely need some modifications and a considerable amount of extra equipment before you are ready to start any serious cruising. New boats bought 'off the shelf' are usually the least equipped of all; you will need a hefty budget allowance to outfit your new acquisition. You will have the gratification of instant ownership (very important to

Custom boats can be built in some unusual locations. This 33 ft (10.6 m) sailing boat is being built in Oman for John and Joan Mc Dermott who intend to cruise back to the UK 'the long way round' when John's tour of duty is completed.

'Now' people) and of course if you choose well, your new boat and its existing equipment should serve you for several years. You should be able to avoid large expenditure on the replacement of major items such as mast(s), rigging, sails, engine and the other equipment that either comes with, or is added to the boat soon after the initial purchase.

Buying a second-hand boat

Buying used is another option, but the purchase of a second-hand boat can be fraught with traps for the unwary. The term *buyer beware* is never more apt than with buying a used boat. If you are able to deal directly with the owner you may avoid some of the pitfalls associated with this type of purchase. There are many honest and trustworthy yacht brokers and boat salespeople handling used boats, however there are also many who have received their sales training selling used cars and the like. You must make sure you are absolutely satisfied before you hand over your money. Always hire a qualified surveyor to check out your boat purchase before you part with *any substantial* amounts of cash.

If you are shopping for a boat away from your home territory you will need to be particularly careful about the ownership rights of the person selling the boat. You would be wise to deal through a local broker with a good reputation; better still use a broker who has affiliations in your home country. To buy a boat dockside from some unknown owner would be the height of folly as many have discovered to their cost.

In the USA boats are often documented (similar to the UK Part 1 Register). In the UK a Part 1 certificate will be a good way of proving ownership; make sure you call the Registrar General's office in Cardiff to check that the document is current. The certificate issued by the Small

Ships Register is not a proof of ownership but it will be a start. Another way to check ownership is to contact the yacht's insurers and the harbour master where the boat is kept.

It is well to remember that at least in the UK, if you buy a boat from a person who does not have legal title to the vessel and it is later reclaimed by its lawful owner, you will most likely be out of pocket and lose your boat and your money. The boat you are considering buying may be subject to a hire purchase agreement, it may form part of a legal dispute or there may be some other impediment in the title. Make sure you carefully check builder's certificates, bills of sale and any other documentation that is offered to prove the current ownership.

Surveys are a must

You will often have to pay for the boat to be hauled out to allow for a full survey. To cut your potential costs, you can conduct a very detailed inspection of the interior, galley equipment, pumps, heating, batteries as well as mast(s), rigging, sails, dinghy and electronic equipment before you commit yourself to a full survey. Do not be rushed, do not be afraid of being a nuisance, take your time. If you have trusted and knowledgeable friends who have a *proven* knowledge of things boating, ask their help and advice at this early stage. Do not ignore advice because you have fallen in love with the boat.

Custom building

Custom building is an exciting way to acquire your cruising boat. This term usually refers to having the boat built and/or mostly completed by a professional builder. For those with some boating experience and a patient disposition, this can be the best way of obtaining the cruising boat of your dreams. You will have the opportunity of being involved from conception to completion of your boat.

If you can manage the project yourself, then there are considerable savings to be made. With some intelligent planning you can end up with a beautiful custom cruising boat for less than the cost of an 'off the shelf' equivalent. You can choose an existing design or have a designer prepare custom plans and patterns. If you are able to source your own engine, mast, rigging, sails, deck hardware, engine and interior fittings, you can save a great deal. Any large chandler or marine hardware store will offer worthwhile discounts in return for the size of order that you will have at your disposal. It may even be worthwhile setting yourself up as a 'boat-building enterprise', this will give you access to trade discounts.

Building from a hull or from plans

Building from a hull and deck kit can be an economical way of acquiring a custom built boat. Many of the cruising boats you will see in far off and exotic locations were completed from a 'hull and deck kit'. If following the footsteps of others is any indication then this is one of the most popular ways to obtain a genuine offshore cruising boat. There are a good selection of hull and deck packages built from glass fibre available. There is also a good choice of steel kits while those in timber are becoming rarer.

Building from plans is the most time-consuming option and one which will require some special skills. If you do not already possess the type of experience that would allow you to build your own boat, then you may be able to acquire the skills you need as the work progresses. If you are already an experienced welder, woodworker or have some knowledge of glass fibre, then there is a greater likelihood that you will be able to build a seaworthy boat.

As steel becomes increasingly popular we are seeing many more cruising boats built by owners and workers who gained their experience in small metal shops. There are many designers around the world who specialise in preparing boat plans and patterns for those who want to create their own boat. The builders of these cruising boats have the advantage of knowing every part of their cruising home. Repairs are easier, quicker and certainly less expensive if you have built the boat yourself.

Choosing the right material

When considering a cruising boat, the two main choices are glass fibre and steel. Choosing the material type can be applied to any of the purchasing options, so before we move on let me recommend my favourite hull and deck material and that is steel for the hull and aluminium for the decks and superstructure. This arrangement puts the strength where you need it and allows weight saving where it will be most advantageous. If your budget does not allow for the above combination then an all steel hull, deck and superstructure would be my choice.

After owning steel boats myself, as well as having access to the records of several hundred others, I can state that a properly built steel vessel requires *less not more* maintenance that boats built from other materials. Another benefit of a metal boat is the protection it offers in the event of a lightning strike.

CHAPTER 2

Choosing the Hull

◆ *Hull construction materials; selecting the hull material and comparisons between glass fibre, steel, or copper nickel* ◆ *Keels and other appendages* ◆ *Hull design terms, formulas and technical considerations and what they mean* ◆ *Draft limitations* ◆ *Rudder types* ◆ *Types of ballast* ◆ *Motor sailer hulls*

In days past one could be excused for thinking that there were as many hull types as there were boats afloat. A visit to any marina will reveal that times have changed; the advent of series glass fibre production has produced rows of almost identical boats. Most of these boats are suitable for local and coastal cruising but very few should be considered for long distance voyaging. It is a fact that most successful long distance cruising boats will not be found at a boat show; the most successful long distance cruising boats are purpose designed and built.

In the mid 1960s I designed and built many one-off, glass fibre cruising boats and still do. In the early 1970s when petroleum products became difficult, and in the case of polyester resins almost impossible, to obtain, I started to design steel boats. In this period (except in Holland) there were very few steel hulled pleasure boats. Today I would estimate that 50 per cent of the offshore cruising boats actually 'out there doing it' have steel hulls and most of these have steel decks and superstructures as well.

MATERIALS

If you are building, having built or purchasing a purpose built cruising boat then you will be able to choose the construction material you prefer. If you are buying a production boat then the chances are that it will have a glass fibre hull and you will live with that choice.

Glass fibre

A well built glass fibre hull can provide the basis for a fine cruising boat. In many cases 'well built' should read custom built. It is a fact that many (most) sailing boats spend much of their life securely tied to a well protected dock and provided they can withstand the occasional coastal sail they are deemed to have fulfilled their role. Unfortunately when considering a boat for serious coastal or offshore cruising one has to assume that sooner or later the boat will have to withstand all that nature can offer.

There are only a few 'production' glass fibre boats that can meet the criteria required to warrant the title of 'serious cruising boat'.

If you are planning to purchase a 'production' glass fibre boat then you may be able to intervene in the building of your boat to the extent of selecting a heavier laminate and additional strengthening than would be the norm for the particular design. I have designed and been involved in the building of many sandwich fibreglass hulls and my preference would be for a single skin hull. Why? It is easier to repair and problems, if any, would be more obvious before they became major issues. The sandwich material does provide some insulation from heat, cold, condensation and sound. You can add suitable insulation inside a single skin hull in the areas where it is required (usually above the waterline).

The main advantages of choosing a cruising boat built from glass fibre are: low maintenance (if buying used, have the hull checked for osmosis); the wide selection of sizes and types available in both new and used models; good resale value (widely accepted by the average weekend sailor); and finally you may not have to defend yourself for owning a steel boat!

Steel

As I mentioned in the previous chapter, when choosing the hull material for a cruising boat, my preference is for steel. The advantages of using steel include: super strength (steel will withstand a grounding or striking a foreign body better than any other hull material); versatility and cost (it is much less expensive to have a steel hull custom built than any other material); ease and cost of repairs (should you have occasion to repair your boat, you will find competent steel workers in all parts of the world). Finally, quite often you will want to modify your existing cruising boat; with steel this is relatively simple. If you

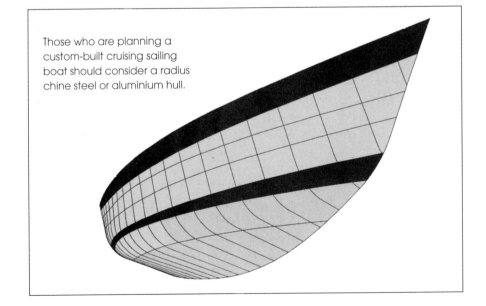

Those who are planning a custom-built cruising sailing boat should consider a radius chine steel or aluminium hull.

are buying a second-hand boat, have the hull thoroughly checked by a competent marine surveyor who has experience of steel construction.

The only disadvantages with steel are perceived rather than actual; for instance you will often be told that steel requires excessive maintenance, not true, a well prepared and painted steel boat will not require attention for several years. Another misconception is that steel is heavy; it is a fact that in the 40 ft (12.19 m) and above size range, a steel boat will weigh the same as a *well built* glass fibre boat of the same length.

Copper nickel

A lesser known but potentially fine hull material is copper nickel; this metal does not rust, is impervious to marine growth and except for cosmetic reasons never needs painting. Several fishing trawlers and a few power and sailing boats have been built from copper nickel and they have been very successful as far as long life and freedom from maintenance is concerned. Although more expensive than steel, copper nickel is worth considering if you are building a new boat that you plan to own for many years.

KEELS

This term covers the part of the hull below the canoe body. The keel may be part of the hull in that the hull sections flow smoothly from keel to hull (sometimes described as a hollow heel). In other cases the keel and hull meet at a definite angle. Keels may be subdivided into long keel, long fin keel, fin keel, drop keel, centreboard keel, wing keel, bulb keel, twin keel and bilge keel. For the purposes of discussion let us consider twin keels as keels that carry ballast and replace a centreline keel. Bilge keels are usually simple plates placed outboard at about 25 per cent waterline beam, and are accompanied by a centre line ballasted main keel.

When you start considering what type of boat will best serve your particular requirements, you will need to decide, whether you prefer a long or short keel hull. There are a variety of sub-types within the two broad definitions. Maximum draft will be an important consideration and this is one of the first subjects raised by most clients when they are considering a stock or custom design. Unless you are planning to undertake most of your cruising in particularly shoal waters, you should consider the 'one fathom line' when deciding on a suitable draft for your boat. As one fathom equals 6 ft (1.83 m), we can assume that any draft under 6 ft or say 2 m is a reasonable compromise. Considering draft versus length of hull, you can assume that most hulls with a LOA of under 50 ft (15.24 m) can be arranged to accommodate a draft of 6 ft (1.83 m) or less.

It is our experience that drop keels or centreboards do not make ideal cruising partners. On the KISS principle, it is easy to see that any keel that requires constant attention, as in the case of drop keels and centreboards, is particularly vulnerable to damage.

HULL DESIGN TERMS

For the purposes of explaining the various terms related to the hull, assume the hull includes the keel, skeg and other appendages. Often when one speaks of the hull, we also mean the decks and superstructure. In this chapter we are concentrating on the hull only and other areas will be covered later.

Listed in this chapter are some of the terms you will encounter when discussing various hull forms. If you are already knowledgeable in these names and their meanings then feel free to surf through this section.

LINES PLANS

Understanding the water lines is always important and especially if you are building a new boat or buying new and have access to a set of hull lines. This set of drawings is commonly referred to as *the lines plan*. To fully understand the content takes considerable experience, however there is much vital information that can be understood by all. A lines plan generally consists of three views of the hull; body plan, profile and plan view. The hull is bisected by the stations, water lines and buttocks; see accompanying drawings.

By studying the lines and relating these to the hydrostatic information that normally accompanies the drawings, you will be able to learn a considerable amount about how the boat will perform in a variety of conditions under both sail and power. If you do not have the experience to make some sense out of this information then seek the help of a knowledgeable friend. If you have engaged the services of a naval architect or qualified yacht designer then you should act on his or her advice; it would not be polite to seek advice from another designer. If you don't trust the judgement of your chosen professional, change to another.

CANOE BODY

This refers to the main part of the hull excluding the keel and skeg and is sometimes used by designers for separate calculations with or without the keel attached. The canoe body can be *flat floored* (relatively flat on the bottom) or moderately *veed* throughout its length.

CANOE STERN

This term is used to describe a certain type of stern. The true canoe stern would be more pointed than a stern so described today, and even a stern best described as having a golf ball shape, is sometimes called a canoe stern. Also referred to as a *double ender*, this type of hull is not as popular as it was 10 to 15 years ago.

TRANSOMS

Although not strictly accurate in nautical terminology, the terms stern and transom are often used to describe the aft end of the hull. Not all sterns have transoms. Most sailing boats today have either a traditional transom or reverse transom stern. One relatively recent development is the advent of the 'sugar scoop' stern which incorporates a vertical transom within a reverse angle ending to the hull. This arrangement usually features steps for re-boarding from the water or when the boat is moored stern-to in European fashion.. The reverse transom is also often fitted with boarding steps that are built into the transom itself.

LENGTH

This should be a simple indication of the size of a hull in at least one dimension, however

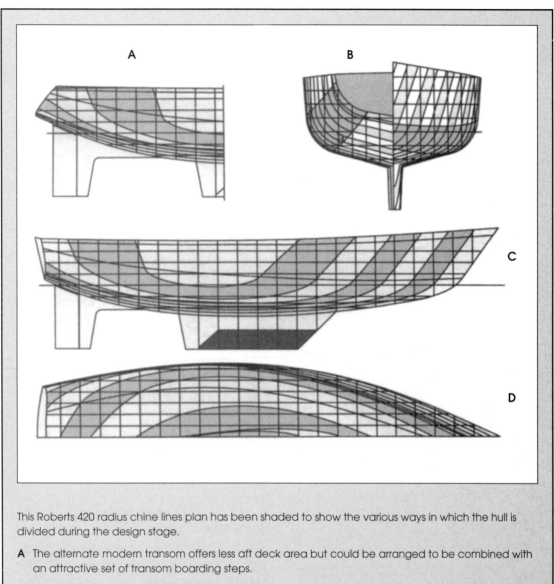

This Roberts 420 radius chine lines plan has been shaded to show the various ways in which the hull is divided during the design stage.

A The alternate modern transom offers less aft deck area but could be arranged to be combined with an attractive set of transom boarding steps.

B The sections of frames are drawn at half stations, some lines plans only have 10 to 14 stations. The shaded radius chine section shows the constant radius of 2 ft 3 ins (838 mm) but the amount of arc will vary from greatest at the stern to the smallest at the bow.

C On the profile view the 1 ft (305 mm) equally spacd buttock lines are picked out by shading each alternate area. These lines are used in fairing the lines and when viewed by an experienced eye can be used to reveal much about the hull form of the particular design. Note the generous proportioned skeg and fence ahead of the rudder.

D This plan view gives a clear indication of the waterlines that are spaced at 1 ft (305 mm) through the profile (C). Note the borttom of the radius chine running through a lower unshaded waterline.

HULL DESIGN TERMS continued

even this simple term can be confusing. The terms *length over all* (LOA) and *length over deck* (LOD), are often confused. Length overall in its true meaning is the actual length of the hull including bowsprit or bumpkin and any other items that extend beyond the hull. Often the term LOA is used to express the length of the hull only; this is incorrect and our own design office has been guilty of this misla-belling. Sometimes a design has several sail plans and these involve bowsprits of different lengths so it is more accurate to ignore these items when stating the length.

Make sure you understand the true length of the hull; in its true expression it should read LOD or *length over deck*. There is another associated term, LPD, *length between perpendiculars*, which is often used to describe the length of the hull when boats are 'built to class' such as Lloyds rules, the American Bureau of Shipping or the more recently introduced European Boating Directive. This measurement indicated in a brochure or advertisement, is usually the same as LOD. One sure way to ascertain just what you are getting for your money is to measure the boat yourself.

WATERLINE LENGTH

This measurement is usually expressed as LWL or DWL *load or designed waterline length*. The waterline runs from where the bow enters the water to where the stern or aft canoe body and the water meet. The designer usually shows it from station 0 to station 10. This is the designer's educated guess of where the waterline will come to on the hull. Many boats are advertised with a stated displacement and waterline length that may not be relevant to the actual boat cruising in trim. (See also Displacement below.)

BEAM and WATERLINE BEAM

These are BOA and WB respectively. Beam overall or beam (max), are used to express the widest part of the hull; usually at the sheer or deck line and near the longitudinal centre of the hull. A boat with tumblehome is one where the widest beam is below the sheer or deck. WB or BW expresses the widest beam at the waterline, usually located a little aft of the location of the widest BOA.

DRAFT

This measurement represents how much the hull draws, or in simpler terms the amount of hull and appendages that will be under the water. In the case of a centreboard or drop keel hull there will be usually two measurements shown, one to represent the draft with the keel raised and the other for the maximum draft with the keel or centreboard in the down position. In the case of a fixed keel boat the draft will include the keel. The draft may vary depending on the loading of the hull, number of crew, state of the fuel and water tanks and the amount of stores on board, etc.

DISPLACEMENT

The true displacement of the hull is the actual weight of the entire boat including the ballast keel, stores, water, fuel, equipment and crew. Usually the true displacement (when known) will be shown in long tons (2240 lb = 1 long ton) or tonnes, kilograms or even in cubic feet (35 cu ft of sea water = 1 long ton). As fresh water weighs only 62.4 lb per cu ft, your boat will draw more in fresh water. The reason that the true displacement figure rarely appears in reviews and published information about most sail boats is that *light displacement* has

HULL DESIGN TERMS continued

been held as a virtue in some quarters. I do not agree but consider moderately heavy displacement to be a desirable feature for a cruising vessel. Within certain limitations, the heavier the designed displacement, the more stores, water and fuel the boat can carry without adversely affecting the performance. The worst combination is an overloaded light displacement sailing cruiser. (See also Displacement length ratio below.)

CENTRE OF BUOYANCY and CENTRE OF GRAVITY

Usually shown respectively as CB and CG, these terms refer to the centre of the displacement of the hull. If the hull is to float level as designed, then the CB must be directly over the centre of gravity (CG). The boat will change trim until the actual CB is over the CG. For example if you add items such as a new water tank, heavy anchor chain or davits, then you will change the centre of gravity of the boat and the trim will change until the CB is directly over the CG.

CENTRE OF FLOTATION

Usually expressed as CF, this is the centre of the *area* of the waterline. If you take a slice through the hull exactly on the waterline and then find the centre of the area of that section then that is the CF of the hull. On most hulls the location is a little aft of the CB and like the CB the CF is usually shown as a distance aft of the bow or as a percentage of the waterline aft of station 0.

POUNDS PER INCH IMMERSION or KILOS PER CENTIMETRE IMMERSION

These are shown respectively as PP/I or K/CM.

These terms indicate the weight in either pounds or kilograms required to sink the hull evenly in the water either one inch or one centimetre. In almost all hulls as the hull widens above the DWL so the number increases proportionally as the hull sinks past its designed waterline.

WETTED SURFACE

Shown as WS, this indicates the wetted surface area of the hull below the waterline. Some designers place great importance on this figure stating that the greater the surface area of hull that has to be pushed through the water the less the performance that can be expected. As there are many other factors that contribute to the overall performance of a cruising boat you should not put too much importance on this number.

PRISMATIC COEFFICIENT

Usually indicated as PC or CP this is a figure that represents the underwater portion of the hull as follows; if you take a block of wood that has the maximum length, width and depth of the hull with the shape of the midsection carved throughout its length and then carve the underwater shape of the hull from this block; the CP is the relationship of the volume of the finished block to the block originally carved to the midsection shape throughout. The number represents the fullness of the ends of the hull. The more you carve away the ends the smaller the PC number. PCs can range from just below 0.50 for a fine racing hull through to 0.70 or more for a motorboat. Most sailing cruisers will have PCs that fall between 0.53 and 0.59

HULL DESIGN TERMS continued

CENTRE OF LATERAL PLANE or
CENTRE OF LATERAL RESISTANCE

Known as CLP or CLR these terms refer to the *geometric* centre of the underwater profile of the hull. If you were to attach a line to this exact point and tow the hull sideways then the hull should move through the water without turning one way or the other. This calculation is used when laying out a sail plan.

CENTRE OF EFFORT

Known as CE, this is the other equation needed by the designer when matching the sail plan to the hull. The CE is the geometric centre of the sail plan usually calculated by adding the area of the fore triangle and the main (and mizzen if present) and calculating the centre of all sails. It is usual to place the CE of the sail plan ahead of CE. The amount of lead depends on many factors, and these calculations are best left to an experienced designer.

DISPLACEMENT LENGTH RATIO

Commonly called the D/L ratio it is calculated by taking the displacement in tons and dividing by 0.01 DWL cubed or Dt / (0.01 DWL)3 or as follows:

$$D/L \text{ ratio} = \frac{\text{Displacement in long tons}}{(0.01 \text{ DWL}) 3}$$
$$(2240 \text{ lbs} = 1 \text{ long ton})$$

The resulting figure can compare the fullness of hulls. Each designer has his or her own pet theory as to the ideal D/L ratio for boats intended for different purposes. The ratio may vary depending on the waterline length so one has to consider this figure only in conjunction with other factors. For most cruising boats the D/L figure usually lies between 280 and 420, cruising boats need adequate *designed* displacement. Overloaded cruising boats will have heavy displacement whether you like it or not, so make sure your cruising boat was designed to carry the large loads that form part of any cruising experience.

RESISTANCE

While you will be relying on the wind to drive your boat in the desired direction, there are many other related factors working against your intentions. One speed limiter is wind resistance caused by the wind drag on areas such as hull topsides, superstructures, mast(s) and boom(s), rigging etc. While racing yachtsmen are always searching for slimmer spars and rigging and lower profile hulls and similar areas of drag reduction, these options are often not viable with cruising boats. There are many other areas of your boat which cause resistance, for example skegs, feathered or free-wheeling propellers etc. In all cases you will need to weigh up the benefits of reduced resistance over loss of living space, ultimate strength and other desirable features of a successful cruising boat.

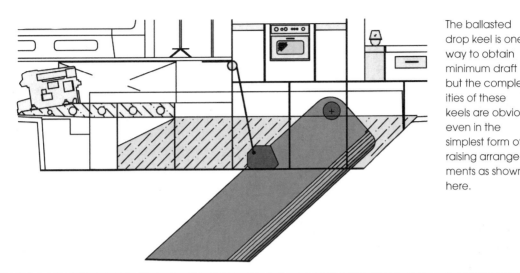

The ballasted drop keel is one way to obtain minimum draft but the complexities of these keels are obvious even in the simplest form of raising arrangements as shown here.

KEEL GLOSSARY

- *Root chord* Horizontal line at the top of the keel span or length along the top of the keel where it joins canoe body.
- *Tip chord* Horizontal line at bottom of the keel span or length of bottom of keel.
- *Span* Distance between root chord and tip chord or simply the depth.
- *Mid-span foil* Shape of foil at halfway span or shape of foil halfway down the keel.
- *Vertical CG of ballast* Vertical location of the centre of gravity of the ballast.
- *Leading edge sweep angle* The leading edge angle measured from the vertical.
- *Trailing edge angle* Angle of the trailing edge measured from vertical, may be positive (top aft) or negative (top closer to bow).
- *Aspect ratio* Ratio of keel depth to averaged or mid-span length or D x MS = aspect ratio

Short fin keels

Current thinking amongst the racing fraternity is that a fin keel with a narrow span (fore and aft dimension) and deep draft and with most of the ballast in a bulb, offers the best performance. This type of keel is difficult to engineer and would be easily damaged when going aground. It is virtually impossible to slip in remote areas. Needless to say that a boat fitted with this keel would also be impossible to beach, and it also results in a draft that is too deep for many of the world's most popular cruising grounds. This keel arrangement is totally unsuitable for a cruising boat.

Do not choose a keel that is too thin in section (plan form). Short fins (span or profile view) and thin foil sections (plan view) are normally accompanied by deep draft; all undesirable features in a cruising boat. There are many acceptable foil sections that can be used to design a cruising boat keel. Each boat designer has his or her own pet group of foils and it is not necessary for you to make an in-depth study on the subject.

Long fin keels

When considering a hull with a short keel (suitable ones are generally referred to as a long fin) you should look for one where the keel length at the point where it joins the hull, is between 30 per cent and 40 per cent of the waterline length. For example on a hull with a 30 ft (9.14 m) waterline the root of the keel would measure between 10 ft (3.05 m) and 12 ft (3.66 m). This is only intended as a rule of thumb, as mentioned above, any keel substantially shorter than 30 per cent of the waterline length will have many disadvantages when cruising.

A sailing cruising boat fitted with a fin keel should have a skeg and preferably one that includes a fence (see page 38). Make sure the skeg has a generous fore and aft length where it joins the canoe body. The skeg to hull join can be strengthened (at the expense of a small loss of performance) by the addition of a fillet running fore and aft and at 45 degrees to the canoe body and the skeg.

Bulb keels and flared keels

The bulb keel that I would consider suitable for a cruising boat is not one of those affairs hung on a long (deep) thin (plan form) keel but rather a thickening of the keel at the bottom of a regular short or long fin as described above. The idea of a bulb is to get the ballast down where it will have best effect in adding to the stability of your boat. A bulb need not be a *bulb* but the lower part of the keel can be *flared* to accept more of the ballast down at the bottom of the keel. I have been experimenting with this type of keel and the initial results are promising. The patented *Scheel* keel is another example of this type.

Wing keels

Wing or winglet keels can provide a good way of decreasing the draft, but *unless they are carefully designed* they can be prone to becoming entangled with any stray ropes, sea weed and similar items that may be lurking just below the water. Another problem for those whose boats dry out is that the suction that can be set up between a wing keel and a soft muddy bottom can result in the keel wanting to stay put. Providing you are aboard at the time, rocking the boat side to side can usually overcome this problem. Wing keels should be relatively thick and should be designed so

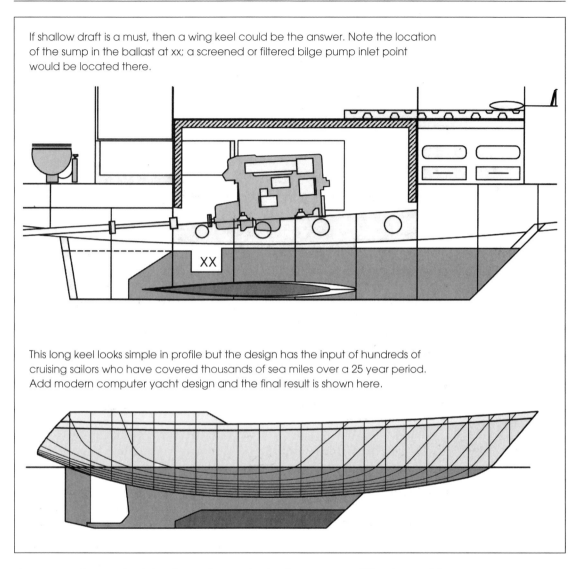

If shallow draft is a must, then a wing keel could be the answer. Note the location of the sump in the ballast at xx; a screened or filtered bilge pump inlet point would be located there.

This long keel looks simple in profile but the design has the input of hundreds of cruising sailors who have covered thousands of sea miles over a 25 year period. Add modern computer yacht design and the final result is shown here.

they are adequately joined to the main keel structure. The long thin versions that are seen on some racing sailboats have no place on any cruiser. Do not rule out a wing keel, just consider the options carefully, before making the decision to incorporate this feature on your boat. A wing keel may be designed so that it is more of a bulb as described above than an actual wing in shape.

Long keels

In the 1970s it seemed that most people considering cruising boats desired a hull fitted with a long keel. There are many types of long keels and some are ideally suited for cruising while others are totally unsuited; some long keels have very bad habits. The traditional long keel had the rudder hung directly off the aft end of the keel that was set at an angle. In order to accommodate the propeller, it was necessary to cut an aperture either in the aft end of the keel or in the forward edge of the rudder or partially in both areas. This arrangement invariably added an undesirable amount of weather helm. The modern 'long keel' embodies a long fin or a full keel as embodied in the Spray range; with a distinct heel extending aft from the bottom of the keel, the rudder is then vertical and supported at the lower end by the heel (see page 35). This latter 'long keel' arrangement where the rudder is further aft and separated from the keel in most cases results in a well balanced hull.

There are three distinct types of long keel and many sub types. However, in my opinion, only two of these main types are suitable for cruising boats.

Firstly, eliminate the undesirable type of long keel; that is one where the aft end of the keel has a considerable rake, sometimes as much as 45 degrees from where the aft end of the keel joins the canoe body. The bottom of the aft end is nearer the bow. Often the rudder is hung directly on the aft end of this keel. The net effect of this arrangement is that the action of the rudder tends to have a twisting rather than a turning motion and expends some of its effort to turn the bow down and stern upwards rather than simply steering the hull.

There are two types of long keel that make excellent cruising partners. The first is typified in the *Spray* hull. This keel is easily identified by the fact that it runs the full length of the hull from the forward end to where it blends into the stem and then drops gradually so that the aft lower end is a greater distance from the waterline than at the forward end. This is a traditional keel arrangement favoured for the past 200 years in fishing boats and other work boats of the past. 'The sea does not change' and any proven and successful hull type is worth consideration, especially when it has evolved over a couple of centuries.

The second long keel type that I favour is best illustrated in the Maurice Griffiths new Golden Hind 34, Tom Thumb 26, Roberts 432 and similar long keel designs. These keels feature a well cut away forefoot to balance the fact that the bottom of the keel is level with the waterline; this all has to do with the area in profile of the keel and the relationship with its fore and aft location relative to the waterline of the hull. If the centre of the area of the keel is too far forward then an undesirable amount of weather helm is almost a certainty.

Another feature of this type of long keel/canoe body combination is the sizable open area between the aft end of the keel and the forward end of the vertical rudder. The resulting large aperture has many advantages including allowing a generous space between the propeller blade tips and the canoe body and the heel. The large aperture provides excellent protection for the shaft and the propeller.

Twin or bilge keels

The term twin keels generally refers to twin-ballasted keels with no centre keel. Bilge keels can be similar but with the addition of a centre keel; the

If you intend to go long-distance cruising in a boat with a skeg, make sure that it is of adequate proportions and up to the job. The steel 44 ft (13.4 m) sailboat pictured here has a substantial skeg although a fence would improve even this beefy structure.

ballast can either be in the centre keel or divided between the three appendages. Bilge plates are often erroneously referred to as bilge keels, however usually this type of arrangement consists of a centre keel containing all of the ballast and twin bilge plates that may be simply bolted on to the hull.

In the early days of twin keels, there were some interesting cases where the twin keels sank into the muddy bottom, a not unusual occurrence with any keel, however in these occasions when the tide rose the keels detached themselves from the hull and remained firmly stuck! Fortunately better construction techniques have eliminated such happenings.

Twin and bilge keels have enjoyed a long popularity in the UK. Due to many of the anchorages and harbours drying out at low tide and in some cases mud berths being the only type of mooring available, this type of keel seemed the answer. Several head to head tests have been conducted where similar hulls were fitted with twin keels, centre keels and centre boards and sailed together. In these tests the single keels usually came off best followed by the centre boarders and with the twin keeler turning in the least impressive performance.

If your cruising routes demand that you have to use 'drying out' moorings and you are worried about some of the other disadvantages of centreboard or drop keel boats, the twin keel configuration may be your best choice.

Skeg

This appendage is located near the aft end of the waterline and ahead of the rudder; its purpose is to enhance the effectiveness of the rudder. Skegs are of varying widths (in profile) but only 10 per cent of the area ahead of the rudder is considered as effective in helping the rudder to steer the vessel; the remainder of the skeg makes an important contribution to the boat's directional stability. Skegs can be vulnerable to damage so they have to be built in such a way as to withstand grounding and being caught in underwater obstructions such as fishing nets. From the mid-seventies to recent times I was a strong supporter of the longish fin keel and skeg combination. There are no doubts about their effectiveness in helping to steer a sailing boat. More recently I have decided that a modified long keel fitted with a substantial heel or shoe combined with a separately hung rudder may be a better option.

Fence

A fence is a worthwhile addition to any skeg, it is a centreline fin that runs between the upper leading edge of the skeg and sometimes as far forward as the aft end of the keel. The object of the fence is to add strength where the skeg joins the canoe body and also to add additional directional stability to the hull. This appendage is sometimes retro-fitted to help correct weather helm.

Heel or shoe

These terms when used in conjunction with the keel refer to the aft extension of the keel which is used to support the lower rudder bearing and forms the aperture between the aft lower part of the keel and the rudder. As mentioned elsewhere, this arrangement is finding favour with more cruising yachtsmen who are familiar with the shortcomings of other keel-aperture-rudder arrangements.

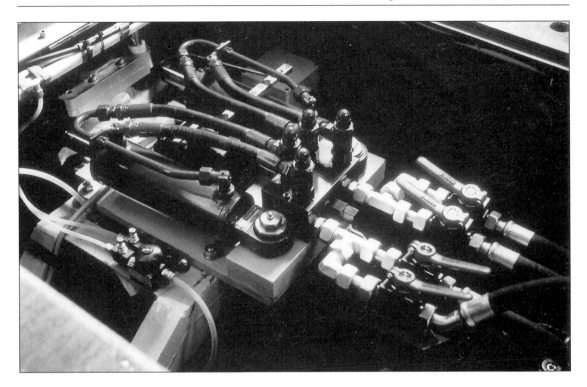

Aperture

Sometimes referred to as the propeller aperture, the aperture is where the propeller shaft and the propeller are often located when the boat is fitted with a skeg or a long keel/heel combination. Apertures can take many forms and in times past they were just large enough to accommodate the propeller with a small clearance all round. If the clearance between the tips of the propeller blades was too small then severe cavitation could result. In designing skegs at one time we used to try and arrange the aperture in the skeg; sometimes this made the skeg weak and vulnerable to damage. It is not a good idea to cut away the rudder to form part of an aperture either. The answer is to have the propeller shaft exit the hull ahead of the skeg, however this removes the protection for the propeller that is a desirable feature for a cruising vessel.

Not all rudder arrangements are as complex as this hydraulic set up on Herbert Fritz's 53 ft (16.1 m) charter sailboat *Kallisto*. The addition of an auto pilot and twin helm locations requires considerable plumbing to achieve an effective fail-safe system.

RUDDER TYPES

The rudder type will often be governed by the keel and transom choices. If your hull has a transom that is located close to the aft end of the waterline then you may consider a transom hung rudder. While this does make a satisfactory cruising arrangement, it is seldom practical because most modern cruising hulls have either a reverse transom or an overhanging stern.

Rudders come in many shapes and sizes and it is worth understanding the terminology before considering which type of rudder is best suited to pointing your cruising boat in the right direction. If your rudder fails, then you may have to consider other methods of steering your boat. Although rudders have been located at just about every possible part of the hull, we will consider only those that are near, or at, the aft end of the waterline.

Transom hung rudder

This is a rudder that is usually attached to or hung on a transom or canoe stern and is attached to the hull by way of pintles and gudgeons. This arrangement has the advantage that it is easy to ship and unship for repair or for allowing the propeller shaft to be removed. To use this rudder you will need a hull where the transom and aft end of the waterline terminate at or near the same point. One disadvantage is that this precludes aft over-hangs which can provide additional waterline length when the boat is heeled. Usually transom hung rudders have a fixed blade but may be combined with one of the shoal draft varieties. (See shoal draft rudder.)

Shoal draft rudders

These rudders are sometimes seen on centreboard or drop keel boats. The bottom half of the rudder is arranged like a kick-up centreboard; the blade will raise itself with or without assistance in the event that the boat is about to go aground. This type of rudder is sometimes found on coastal cruisers that frequently sail in shoal waters. Another version will have a dagger-board blade, similar to a dagger centreboard; the disadvantage of this type is that it can easily be damaged or broken if it is not raised in a timely manner.

Balanced rudder

This is a rudder where a portion, usually between 5 per cent and 10 per cent of the blade area, is ahead of the rudder shaft. The idea is to correct weather helm and/or make the steering lighter. My opinion is that balanced rudders only hide a problem rather than correct it so be cautious when you see a hull with this type of rudder. Another problem with balanced rudders is that when the rudder is turned more than a few degrees, it can act as a brake.

Skeg hung rudder

This is a rudder that is aft of a skeg. The effect of this arrangement is that the skeg enhances the effect of the rudder while providing directional stability and enhanced windward performance. Stay away from arrangements where the skeg is only half the depth of the rudder and the bottom half of the rudder carries some balance; this arrangement is notorious for catching stray ropes and lines and playing havoc with your steering.

Heel or shoe supported rudder

This rudder is usually arranged with the bottom end of the rudder shaft supported in a cup bearing located on the heel. The upper end of the rudder shaft enters the canoe body at around station 10 (aft end of the waterline). This rudder is usually not balanced. The whole arrangement forms a closed box (in profile) where the shaft and propeller are protected from damage from the many objects floating on or near the surface of the sea. This is one of my recommended rudder arrangements for cruising boats.

Twin rudders

These are sometimes used either on twin keel boats or on drop keel types and some cases are combined with twin steering wheels. The idea is that the leeward rudder is always in the optimum location to give maximum steering control. In practice twin rudders are usually more trouble than they are worth.

Spade rudders

As the name suggests these are shaped like a spade and are hung on rudder post or shaft. These rudders usually have 5 per cent to 10 per cent of balance and are often seen on racing sail boats. As these rudders are unprotected by any skeg or heel and are unsupported on the bottom, they are more susceptible to damage than most other types. Not my idea of the ideal cruising rudder. In the rarefied air of racing, these rudders rule supreme; the variety of shapes is only outnumbered by the claims made for some designer's latest creation. Recently spade rudders shaped to mimic a shark's fin (up-side down) was the hottest item; later the designer decided that for optimum performance the aft end of the keel should match the inverted shark's appendage. These ideas seemed to disappear after one season.

HULL ENDS AND OVERHANGS

Over the years there have been many theories as to the best shapes for the ends to the hull and the correct amount of overhang at the bow and the stern. The hull ends refer to the forward end, forward overhang and area about the bow, and the aft hull end generally refers to the area including overhangs and area around the stern.

The period from well before the Second World War through to the 1960s spawned hulls with longish overhangs; extreme examples had a length on deck twice that of the waterline. Many of these boats were designed to a racing or rating rule; the theory was that as the boat heeled it picked up considerable (free) waterline length and so 'beat the rule'. Cruising boats built during this period often mimicked the inshore and

Not all motor sailers are this obvious. The Pacific Coast Fisherman 40 (PCF 40), as its name suggests, is based on a true displacement fishing power boat hull. One recently 'sailed' from Australia to Ireland.

offshore racing boats of the time. The cruiser/racer or racer/cruiser was a product of this type of thinking and as with many other things built to please all, these boats often pleased no one; too slow to make a good racing boat and too wet or otherwise unsuitable for serious cruising.

Fortunately at the present there is a more distinct division between sailing boats designed and built for racing and those designed and built for cruising. Moderate ends are the rule and it has been conclusively proven by thousands of cruising crews that a boat with moderate ends makes the best sea boat.

WATER BALLAST

This type of ballast, as the name suggests, consists of water that is held in tanks usually located towards the sides of the hull. The tanks are connected by one or more large diameter pipes and a pumping arrangement so that the water can be transferred from one side of the boat to the other. The windward side tank is kept full thus adding to the stability of the boat when sailing to windward; on or during tacking the water is transferred to the other side. These arrangements can have some benefit in a trailer sailer or similar small sailboat. The inability to tack quickly, the chances of the boat being unprepared in the event of a sudden wind shift are just two of several reasons why water ballast is unsuitable for any offshore cruiser.

MOTOR SAILER HULLS

The term motor sailer used to mean a boat best described as a 50/50 that is 50 per cent motor and 50 per cent sail. Occasionally one would hear boats referred to as 60/40 or by some similar definition. Today this distinction has been blurred to such an extent that I am not sure the term has any true meaning at all. As it is a term you will encounter when you go out searching for your cruising boat we had best decide what most people mean when they refer to a boat as a *motor sailer*. To add more confusion to the definition of a motor sailer, we now have a similar expression being developed as part of the new (European) EU Boating Directive.

My interpretation of the term motor sailer is best expressed by the Pacific Coast Fisherman 40. The PCF 40 is a motorboat (pure displacement hull, with a fishing boat heritage) that has been fitted with a modest but effective sail plan. I would not recommend this type of boat as a serious long distance passage-making vessel, but rather as one ideal for coastal cruising. Needless to say planing hull power boats are not suitable for conversion to motor sailers; this has been tried by some UK and US boat building companies that should have known better; the results were less than satisfactory.

More recently you are likely to hear the term motor sailer applied to a variety of sailing boats equipped with varying sizes of auxiliary power. Considering the term motor sailer in its more recent usage I would say that a boat fitted with an engine with a capacity of more than 2.5 horse power per 1000 lb displacement (1.82 Kw per 454 kg) might be termed a motor sailer.

You will need to consider the hull form rather than the general terminology, when you are making your decision as to which hull is most suitable for your particular type of cruising. If you are considering cruising the canals of Europe with the odd foray into the Mediterranean, then a motor sailer in its true context could be the right choice for you.

CHAPTER 3

Decks and Superstructures

◆ Deck and superstructure arrangements ◆ Flush or raised decks ◆ Pilot houses ◆ Windows and ports ◆ Hatches ◆ Cockpits ◆ Transoms and bulwarks ◆ Deck coverings ◆ Lifelines, pulpits and pushpits

---

You may already have a favourite deck arrangement: centre or aft cockpit, trunk cabin or flush deck, open cockpit or pilot house. Perhaps you prefer a raised deck either forward, amidships or aft by way of a poop stern. The boat you are considering may have a combination of two or more of these features.

In most boats the same construction material is used for the decks, superstructure and hull. If you are having a boat built or are otherwise in a position to choose the construction material for your deck you may want to vary this convention, but do proceed with caution. One excellent combination is to utilise a special fusion strip to match an aluminium deck and superstructure to a steel hull. For slogging through unknown waters there is nothing like a steel hull; for saving weight, ease of construction and general suitability, aluminium is tops for decks and superstructures. If you cannot afford aluminium then an all steel boat would be my next choice.

PLYWOOD DECKS AND SUPERSTRUCTURES

Using timber and/or plywood to build decks and superstructures is not a good idea; no matter how careful you are at the construction stage you will most certainly have problems in later years. Rot is the problem; I was once forcibly taken to task by a person who read the words 'dry rot' in one of my boatbuilding books; I am still talking about 'dry rot', even though it is usually damp in appearance.

FLUSH DECKS

In the past flush decks were considered by many to be a desirable feature of any cruising boat that was intended to be used for serious offshore

This Roberts 36 features a raised foredeck.

passage making. Most arguments advanced in favour of flush decks were based on the idea that the integrity of the whole hull and deck was better preserved by the elimination of raised cabin sides, short deck beams, trunk cabins and similar structures. This argument could be sustained when boats were built mainly of timber. Today most boats are built of either glassfibre or metal (steel, aluminium or copper nickel) from which it is much easier to build a single homogeneous structure. The development of modern adhesives has improved the structural strength on modern timber boats so even if you choose this material you are not restricted to flush deck or any other arrangement.

Although flush decks are no longer considered an absolute necessity for the ultimate cruising boat, this type of structure can be used to advantage either in part or in total for certain types of boats. The disadvantage of a totally flush decked boat is that in the unlikely event of a 180° total capsize, this type of hull will take longer to right itself than a boat with a cabin structure. Another drawback is that there are less opportunities to install hand holds as installed on most cabin tops. Personally I feel more exposed on a flush-decked hull than on a boat with some superstructure to provide shelter and hand holds as one moves about the deck.

At time of writing the EU Boating Directive is still under development. However I am of the opinion that it will not look kindly on flush-deck designs due to the additional stability when in the *inverted* position. Until the final draft is available we can only speculate as to the influence on future design trends that will be exerted by this legislation.

PARTIAL FLUSH DECKS

A sensibly designed, raised foredeck can add additional room, both actual and perceived, to the fore cabin of any cruising boat. The fore deck should not be so high at the bow so as to interfere with the forward vision of the helmsperson. A step down in the deck height near the bow incorporating a well, can offer protection in an area where you will be handling the anchor and gathering in headsails.

The raised poop stern has gained considerable favour in recent years and thousands of cruising boats feature this arrangement. This structure is usually combined with a centre cockpit and often accompanied by a pilot house. The poop deck is achieved (at the design stage) by simply moving the aft cabin sides to the outside of the hull or by raising the hull sides in this area. One has only to go below on a boat featuring a raised poop stern to appreciate the spacious feeling achieved by this arrangement. The raised poop usually makes it easier to incorporate an *en suite* shower and head, a very desirable feature especially if the crew numbers more than two persons. Another feature often accompanying the poop stern is larger than usual aft cabin windows (one could hardly describe most of them as ports) which are often incorporated into the overall design. (See page 48.)

A few boats are built with a raised deck amidships. In small to medium-sized cruisers this arrangement can add considerable room in the main living area of the hull. Other advantages of this feature could include the extra working area on deck especially around the mast. It may be possible to incorporate a clear stowage space for an upturned dinghy.

PILOT HOUSES

The pilot house or wheel house is known under various names and has been a feature used on all types of boats since time immemorial. Earlier this structure was often referred to as a 'dog house'. The term wheel house is easier to understand. In 1972 a client of mine installed a house of his own design to one of my boats. When I made an adverse remark he replied that he would remove the structure when I took my drawing board outside. Fair comment.

The last 30 years have seen a great rise in the popularity of the pilot house and I cannot imagine designing any boat without including at least one version that incorporated one of these structures. Many boats have pilot houses retro-fitted and this is something you may want to consider when considering purchasing a boat that does not already incorporate this facility. In the past clients have often been somewhat diffident in asking for a pilot house, explaining that the boat was to be used where it was 'too hot', 'too cold' or 'too wet' to do without the security and comfort of this feature. Pilot houses are here to stay and I would not consider owning a boat that did not have one.

Pilot houses can be very short, sometimes no more than a steering shelter; or medium length, closed at the aft end with a lockable door and with steering, navigation and seating for other crew members. They can be long, with considerable accommodation inside usually including steering, dinette, galley etc; in fact a full saloon. I have often seen some so-called pilot houses without steering facilities; in my opinion these 'raised saloons' defeat the whole idea of this desirable feature.

If you are designing your superstructure and intend to include a pilot house, I recommend you start by planning a medium-length version. The steering station will include a comfortable chair for the helmsperson and a generous size opening hatch above the steering station; this is useful for viewing the sails. Provide for a navigation station which may be the main one or an auxiliary one for the helmsperson's use. Include seating for two or more additional crew members.

The forward facing windows can be either regular or reverse sloping and occasionally vertical as seen on some traditional craft. If you look at most fishing boats, you will notice that the forward wheelhouse windows are almost all reverse sloping, the reason for this is that these windows are much less prone to reflections which impair your vision. They are also less likely to need the services of a windscreen wiper as the forward top 'eyebrow' usually keeps most of the rain off. Having lived with both types I would trade the glamour of regular sloping windows for the practical

This 'pilot house' is more of a 'dog house' in that it can be added on after the boat is completed and in the case of damage to this structure, the interior of the boat can still be closed off at the companionway. Note the 'Kent Clearview' (top right of photo). In today's world a windscreen wiper might be more useful.

aspects of the reverse sloping variety. Electric wipers are a nice feature and recommended if your budget will support the expense.

If you are building a new boat make sure that the cabin and wheelhouse sides slope in at least 10 per cent otherwise they can look as though they lean out, which does not look good. There is one notable UK design where the sides do actually slope outwards, enough said!

On the subject of superstructure styling, do not allow any new boat you are building to be too extreme in this area. In a few years when you want to move up, down or out of boating you may find you have difficulty or are unable to dispose of your vessel.

PORTS AND WINDOWS

The larger areas of glass usually associated with poop sterns and the windows in pilot houses will also need careful consideration. In practice larger windows have proved satisfactory provided they are of reasonable proportions and glazed with heavy safety glass, Perspex®, Lexan® or similar material. Needless to say larger windows must have adequate framing. Windows that often appear large are not always large at all; these can be small areas of window backed up with a (sometimes disguised) system of framing. If you feel that the openings in your boat are of such a size as to present a safety hazard then you should carry plywood shutters. If they are required the speed and ease of fitting may be crucial to the safety of your boat. In all cases you should have the ability to close off the openings in case of breakages.

Most boats have at least six regular portlights and these can vary in size and shape and may be fixed (non-opening) or have the ability to open. Opening ports are notorious for leaking so if you can live with fixed ports you will have a drier boat. Ventilation is best arranged by opening cabin top or deck hatches which are easier to keep watertight due in part, to their accessibility and location on the boat.

HATCHES

Hatches are now usually built with aluminium frames and are glazed with tinted plastic or safety glass. The modern hatch will provide more light than any number of portlights could ever do. You will need hatch covers to be used in hot weather. Do not stint on the quality of these hatches, in the event of extreme weather conditions the integrity of your boat may depend on them. If you are fitting out a steel boat then steel framed hatches may be appropriate. Regular hatches come with all forms of opening arrangements including forward opening, aft opening, forward and aft opening. It is wise to have one hatch in each compartment that is large enough to allow any member of the crew to exit in an emergency. Hatches should be capable of being opened firstly from inside, preferably from outside as well and should be fitted with a suitably strong locking device to keep intruders out. Some manufacturers have a line of hatches which are not glazed and are ideal in areas such as the fore deck where they will be subjected to maximum loading. If you are fitting new hatches, check with other owners before you settle on any one type; a leaky hatch is one of the most annoying items on any boat.

I have seen one special ventilation hatch that opens in all four directions plus straight upwards; this hatch did not open to allow crew to exit, but might be useful set in a pilot house top or similar location.

Sliding companionway hatches need special attention. There are a few proprietary ready-made examples available; however it is likely that you will have to fit a custom made one on any boat intended to be used for serious offshore cruising. The main hatch will usually be part of the main entrance and exit to and from your boat and as such should be capable of being secured against unauthorised entry. Unfortunately secured does not mean a simple locking arrangement but more likely a hatch and companionway arrangement that will deter all but the most determined intruder.

COCKPITS

Cruising boats were not always fitted with this feature, in fact a few still manage without them. Most of us prefer the security, both real and perceived, offered by a well designed self-draining cockpit. These work particularly well when combined with protective coamings and comfortable seating. The dimensions of this arrangement are most important and can influence the safety and comfort of the boat in many ways. It is desirable but not always possible to have the cockpit seats measure 6 ft 6 in (2 m) long; this allows a person to lie full length. The width of the well may be best arranged so a person can rest one or both feet on the seat opposite; this generally means a 2 ft (610 mm) or 2 ft 3 in (686 mm) wide well; the depth is best at 1 ft 6 in (457 mm). Seats should be between 1 ft 3in (381 mm) and 1 ft 6 in (457 mm) wide and for comfort behind your knees, rounded on the inboard edge.

The height of the seat back that usually forms part of the coaming will vary depending on the design; however about 2 ft (610 mm) seems to work out well for most people. All cockpits should be self-draining with two separate outlets of generous size, minimum 2 in (100 mm) diameter. The cockpit drains should be fitted with sea cocks that can be closed when required. Finally you should have a reasonable view forward when seated in the cockpit; this easier said than achieved especially if there is a pilot house ahead of your cockpit.

The choice between centre and aft cockpit is usually governed by your choice of interior layout. This choice has become blurred with the advent of staterooms fitted beneath and around an aft cockpit.

TRANSOMS

If your boat is fitted with a 'regular' transom, and if you fit an aft boarding ladder, make sure it hangs vertically when in use; many ladders can swing under the boat when you attempt to use them and this makes it difficult for a person to climb back on board. The best transom ladders have treads rather than just pipe rungs. In bare feet it is difficult to climb a pipe step even if it is sheathed in plastic tube.

Transom steps or 'Sugar scoop' sterns are considered here because they form an extension to the deck and superstructure and cockpit layout. For many years the reverse transom stern did little for the cruising boat except mimic the earlier racing designs and give the boat a 'racier' appearance. Several designers have laid claim to designing the first transom steps but whoever came up with the idea deserves our heartfelt thanks. Transom steps can be coupled with a boarding ladder if you find that the first step in the transom is too high to reach from the water. It takes very careful design to arrange the transom so it is just clear of the water to make boarding easier and yet still retain enough clearance on all angles of sail and not cause a 'rooster tail' with the attendant drag.

BULWARKS

Bulwarks or at least a decent toe rail are usually found on any cruising boat. Bulwarks of varying heights are easily arranged on boats built of most materials, so if you are planning a new boat give this item your earnest consideration. Bulwarks can range in height from say 6 in (150 mm) to 3 ft 3 in (1000 mm); usually the larger the boat the higher the

The cockpit on this Roberts 310 features a raised helmsman's seat and the desirable 'T' shaped well.

bulwark can be without affecting the boat's performance. Traditionally styled boats can take higher bulwarks without spoiling their appearance. Boats as small as 25 ft (7.6 m) LOA can have a 4–6 in (100–150 mm) bulwark and 40 ft (12.19 m) boats look fine with one that is 1 ft 3 in (308 mm) above the deck.

The height of a bulwark is dictated by the proportion of the boat's length to its hull topsides, and this is one item that you must check with the designer of your boat before making changes. You will have to balance the height of the bulwark against the location of the side decks as they affect the interior accommodation. For example can a seat be sited under the deck and still provide sitting headroom?

DECK COVERINGS

Your deck will need some form of treatment to provide a non-slip footing as you move about the boat. If your boat is glass-fibre then it may have a 'non-skid' pattern moulded into it; however I have yet to see a satisfactorily moulded glass-fibre non-skid arrangement on any boat.

The least expensive treatment to make a deck safe to walk on, is to apply a special paint which contains a grit to provide the non-skid surface. Many steel boats use this paint/grit combination and provided it is installed in a proper manner it can work well and still look attractive. When installing a

The deck of this steel 53 ft (16.1 m) cruiser *Kallisto* and occasional charter boat has non-slip deck covering which has already proved itself over several thousand miles of hard usage including a total circumnavigation.

painted non-skid surface you should leave small borders around various fittings and alongside the cabin, inside the bulwark etc., which do not have the grit added. Be careful how you lay out these un-gritted areas as you do not want to leave skid inducing shiny spaces in high traffic areas. If the un-gritted areas are no more than 1¼ in (320 mm) wide around any feature then you should not have a problem; you can always fill in any problem spaces with gritted paint.

The next step up in cost and appearance is to use a deck covering like 'Treadmaster' or a similar product. These coverings are composite materials formed in patterned sheets suitable for gluing to your deck. When laying out this covering you should use a similar pattern as suggested for painting decks with gritted material. Available in a range of attractive colours, these products are bonded to your deck with a special glue that is complementary to the particular product you are installing.

The diamond pattern on some of these sheet products can be hard on your bottom or other areas that may come into contact with the deck; do not use it on cockpit seats or similar locations. There are alternative less harsh patterns that can be used where a user-friendly non-slip surface is required.

At the top of the desirable decking material league is a laid teak deck. Teak is used on the best laid decks; however there are other suitable species of timber that can be used for this purpose. In Australia the local beech is often used and I have seen Douglas fir laid decks in vessels built in the USA. The advantages of a laid deck are that it provides a sure footing when wet or dry, it offers additional insulation, and gives your boat a 'finished look' adding to the resale value by at least as much as the original cost of the decking. If you can afford it, teak is the best.

As the laid deck is almost always installed over a substrate deck, the teak can vary in thickness from ¼ in (6 mm) or less to 1 in (25 mm). The method of fixing the teak deck will vary depending on the material used to build the regular deck. If you are building a new boat then you can sometimes allow for the strength and thickness of the teak when specifying the scantlings for the substrate deck. On a light to medium displacement timber or glass fibre boat to avoid adding excessive weight, you may wish to use full size scantlings for the regular deck and then install thinner teak decking set in epoxy. On a boat with steel decks and in most other cases, I prefer to see a minimum of ⅝ in (15 mm) of teak used; my own boat had a wealthy previous owner and it came with a 1 in (25 mm) thick beautifully installed teak deck. Laid decks can give one an unequalled pride of ownership.

LIFELINES, PULPITS AND PUSHPITS

A lifeline is rightly considered a necessity on any cruising boat. The height is very important, 3 ft (914 mm) above the deck is about right, but this would look too high on many smaller boats. If you have a bulwark then some of the height will be absorbed in this feature and the lifeline stanchions are only needed to make up the remaining height. The 2 ft (609 mm) stanchions that are fitted to many boats are too low to be of any practical use and can cause adult crew members to overbalance.

If your boat is over 35 ft (10.5 m), and especially if it has a traditional appearance, then you may want to consider stainless steel or galvanised/painted pipe lifelines in place of the usual wire. One arrangement I can recommend is to have pipe stanchions and upper rail of the same material and the centre line can be of coated wire. On most modern production sailing boats, lifelines consist of regularly spaced stanchions with two plastic covered wires running fore and aft from pulpit to pushpit. Small rigging screws or turnbuckles are used to tension the lines which are led through eyes in or on the stanchions. This arrangement may be adequate for local sailing but would be totally inadequate if you intend to have children on board, in which case a netting right around the perimeter of the deck will be necessary.

To avoid people using the stanchions as hand holds when boarding and leaving your boat, you should arrange a boarding opening with special reinforced stanchions. In any case make sure they are not only of sufficient dimensions and strength to withstand the weight of a fully grown person being thrown against them but also that they are strongly secured to the deck and/or bulwark. A stanchion that is secured to the deck as well as to the top of the bulwark will be the strongest.

The height of the pulpit and pushpit should match the lifelines but in any case it should be a minimum of 3 ft 3 in (1 m) above the deck; where the lifelines are lower than I have recommended, you should make the pulpit and pushpit a little higher without spoiling the appearance of your boat. If you have steps in the transom then you will most likely want a gate in the pushpit.

CHAPTER 4

The Rig

◆ *Choosing a sail plan for cruising* ◆ *Traditional or modern rigs* ◆ *Junk rigs* ◆ *Bowsprits* ◆ *Standing rigging* ◆ *Masts and spars* ◆ *Winches, cleats and fairleads* ◆ *Sails and reefing* ◆ *Storm sails* ◆ *Self-steering devices*

The past few years have seen a quiet revolution in the number and style of rigs available for cruising sail boats. Although you may have a favourite arrangement in mind, you should at least study the options, several of which you may not have previously considered.

One of your first decisions will be the number of masts required to carry your selected sail plan. Although this decision is somewhat tied to the particular type of rig you prefer, there are overlaps in size where you could choose one, two or more masts and still have an efficient rig.

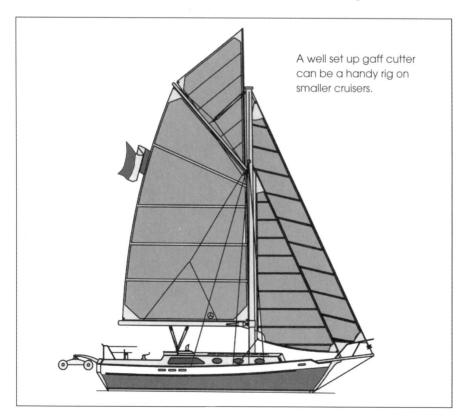

A well set up gaff cutter can be a handy rig on smaller cruisers.

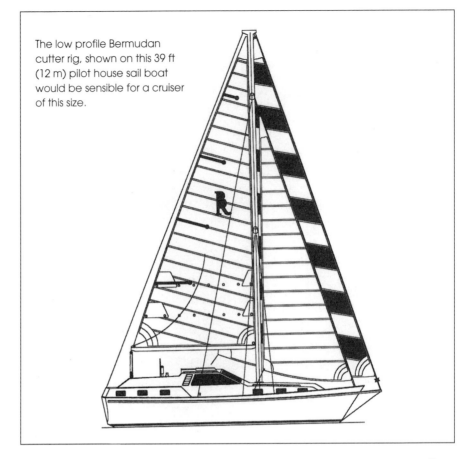

The low profile Bermudan cutter rig, shown on this 39 ft (12 m) pilot house sail boat would be sensible for a cruiser of this size.

In the past I have tended to recommended a single mast (usually a masthead Bermudan cutter) for boats up to 40 ft (12.19m) LOA. The single masted cutter rig used on this size of boat usually results in a mainsail of under 500 sq ft (46.45 sq m) and the headsails will also be of such a size that the weakest member of the crew with the assistance of winches, can raise, lower and sheet the sails. On boats over 45 ft (13.71 m) I tend to recommend two-masted configurations, this will keep all of the individual sail sizes to manageable proportions. Between 40 ft and 45 ft (12.19 m and 13.7 m) is a grey area where either arrangement would be viable. Many builders and owners choose to install rigs well outside these parameters; for instance there are many Roberts 36 ketches and an equal number of Roberts 53s rigged as cutters. Since the early 1960s I have preferred cutter-headed arrangements for both single-masted cutters and ketches.

When considering purchasing or building a cruising boat check the height of the boom(s). The height should be such that when any crew member is standing in the cockpit and if practical also on the side decks all booms will clear his or her head. Although it is not always possible to achieve absolute safety, it is well to remember that many crew have been knocked over the side by a wildly swinging boom.

Jib booms are another potential source of problems, and the benefits, such as automatic tacking of the staysail, or a non-overlapping single headsail, are somewhat offset by the potential danger to life and limb, especially when working on the foredeck after dark. Conversely if you have a jib boom you may have less occasion to go forward in dark or daylight hours.

TRADITIONAL RIGS

This is a good time to consider whether you prefer gaff or any other rig to power your cruising hull. Do not become so enamoured with one style that you insist on using it no matter how unsuitable it is for your type of boat. Apart from ending up with a totally unsuitable rig you could find your boat is unsaleable when you decide to move up or down in size or finally move ashore.

If you choose a traditional style of boat similar to an English style pilot cutter, a Spray type, a Bawley or barge yacht, the gaff rig can make a very satisfactory cruising companion. To install a free standing carbon fibre rig on one of these traditional boats would be a very unsatisfactory arrangement from the practical, common sense and aesthetic points of view. For example, a successful carbon-fibre masted rig usually depends on the hull being easily driven, not overly stiff and capable of good acceleration and this type of boat heels easily before taking up its sailing angle.

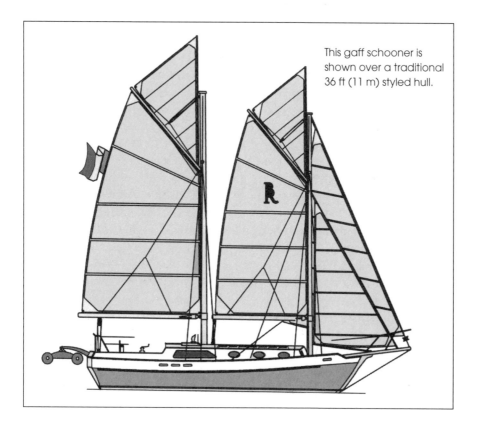

This gaff schooner is shown over a traditional 36 ft (11 m) styled hull.

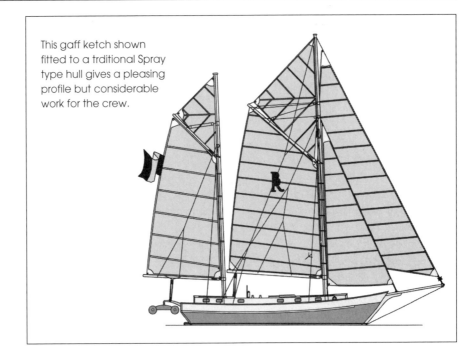

This gaff ketch shown fitted to a trditional Spray type hull gives a pleasing profile but considerable work for the crew.

Lovers of the gaff rig often wish to combine this with the schooner layout. Again traditional boats can be matched up with this arrangement often creating a profile unmatched in beauty by any other rig. Part of the pleasure of owning a cruising or any other type of boat is 'pride of owner-ship': all of the owners of schooners I ever met are very proud of their boats.

If you choose a gaff rig it is a good idea to try and minimise the weight aloft; for instance if you install solid naturally grown timber masts then you may use laminated hollow timber for the gaff spar and perhaps for the boom as well.

Another arrangement that can prove satisfactory is the Bermudan schooner. This rig can come in a variety of arrangements. It is not uncommon to see schooners with gaff foresails and Bermudan mains or conversely, gaff mains and Bermudan foresail. Another well tried rig is the Bermudan staysail schooner, that is Bermudan main and one staysail between the masts backed up by a fisherman sail set above the staysail.

Almost all the rigs discussed here and elsewhere are best arranged with the cutter-headed arrangement of two headsails.

Many owners enjoy a long association with gaff-rigged boats, while others, attracted to the rig by its beauty and charm, are unable to handle the extra work and maintenance required. One advantage of the gaff rig is that it can be much less expensive to install than a modern rig and many traditional boats accept the less expensive gear and 'look right'. The gal-vanised fittings and natural fibre cordage are in keeping with the overall appearance of the boat; expensive stainless steel fittings could look out of place. A well designed gaff rig will accept a natural grown timber mast and boom; fortunately there are still places where you can select your own spars from the forest. In the case of Spray replicas and Spray types, these have been successfully rigged as Bermudan cutters and ketches as well as just about every other rig in existence.

MODERN MASTHEAD RIGS

To most people this rig represents the most convenient and reliable arrangement for a cruising boat sailed by a family crew. You could think of this as a square form of rigging; the forestay, backstay and the cap shrouds all go to the masthead thus squarely supporting the mast in four directions. Depending on the height of the mast, it is divided into either two or three panels where spreaders are located. From near the roots of the spreaders, shrouds are led to the chainplates. The lower shrouds are usually set in pairs led forward and aft of the mast.

A cruising boat fitted with a Bermudan cutter masthead rig, single mast cutter or cutter-headed ketch, is best arranged with two or more sets of spreaders on the main mast. A requirement for most cutters is running

The sloop rig is shown on this modern 46 ft (14 m) design. For long distance cruising, a cutter rig is preferred by many experienced crews.

back stays that are best arranged so that the upper end joins the mast just below the upper set of spreaders and the inner foresail (staysail) tang. The angle of the runner and the location where it meets the deck will need careful consideration; the standard practice is to make the angle at the top end match the angle of the inner or staysail forestay. If the angle is adjusted (reduced) so that both runners may be left set up when short tacking, then this has a definite practical advantage for short-handed sailing. You should consult the designer of your boat, before making any changes.

In the case of conventionally stayed Bermudan rigs it has always been my practice to design these with all of the upper and lower shrouds brought right to the outer edge of the side decks as opposed to narrowing the rig by bringing the lowers inboard to the cabin sides. The advantages of the narrower rigging at the lower ends is that it allows the crew to move about the side decks without ducking under the shrouds. This is sometimes offset by the absence of a suitable anchoring point at the cabin side to take the high loads that are generated by the lowers. In broad beam boats it is possible to get a wide enough base for the lower shrouds to terminate on the cabin sides; however if you rig any boat in this manner you must have a chainplate that is attached to a bulkhead or other strong point that in itself has the necessary strength to accept the high loads.

Fractional rigs

Lovers of lighter displacement cruising boats sometimes prefer the fractional rig. This is usually arranged as a Bermudan sloop (there is not room for two headsails) and the headsail can be smaller and usually reaches up the mast to a location   or ¾ of the distance from the deck. One supposed advantage is that with a larger mainsail, the size of the headsail is reduced. Fractional rigs are generally more fragile than their masthead equivalents and in my opinion are not recommended for an offshore cruising boat.

Back in the mid 1960s when modern masthead rigs were becoming established for both racing and cruising boats, the   and ¾ versions were tried and found to be less desirable than a full masthead arrangement. The modern fractional rig is race bred, and mainly intended to allow the mast to be bent from the top to give more control over the sails, especially the main. With this arrangement the forestay and the cap shrouds all terminate at the ¾ or   location and the backstay is the only stay that extends to the top of the mast. The fractional rig results in the spreaders being angled backward as much as 30°. The cap shrouds are led over the tips of the spreaders and down to the chainplates. The fractional rig is based in part on the 'minimalist' theory that in the case of windage, less is best; this may be fine on a raceboat where a large crew is available to maintain and operate the rig, however on a cruising boat with minimum crew, it is often necessary to expect the rig to look after itself.

It is well to remember that the stiffer cruising boat requires a stronger rig. This fact was very forcibly brought home to early designers of large cruising multihulls. Some of these boats were more heavily built and carried greater amounts of stores etc. than their racing counterparts. When too lightly rigged, many were dismasted despite the wide staying base provided for their rigs. Single-hulled moderate to heavy displacement cruising boats which may heel as little as 10° in anything under a full gale, are typical of boats where an overstrength mast and rigging is recommended.

The science of matching the rig to the hull is best left to an experienced designer; there are so many interrelated factors where an owner could easily make the mistake of mismatching hull and rig thus creating a potentially expensive and dangerous situation. Here we are outlining some of the options but before you make changes to an existing boat or design I recommend you contact the original designer or if that is not possible then seek advice from a suitably qualified person.

Free standing rigs

These modern rigs sometimes called 'Cat' rigs or in the case of a boat with two masts referred to as a 'Cat ketch' or 'Cat schooner', are worth your consideration when one counts the number of possible failure points on a

The Roberts 420 can be rigged as a Cat schooner. Note the absence of shrouds and stays – some Cat rigs are now using a minimum of standing rigging.

The owner of this 25-footer decided to try the junk rig before building a larger cruising boat.

stayed mast; on the average 40 footer (12 m) the number is over 50. Add up the turnbuckles, swages, toggles and other items where a breakage could cause your rig to collapse and you will see why some owners are becoming interested in this option.

JUNK OR LUG RIGS

The Chinese have used these rigs on the rivers and for coastal cruising for thousands of years. What is not so well known it that in the not-so-distant past these junks were much larger and used for long-distance passage making voyages.

Some 35 years ago Englishman Colonel H G 'Blondie' Hasler developed a simplified and modernised version of the traditional junk rig and used it on *Jester* a boat that was to prove the worth of Hasler's junk rig designs. During the past few years, hundreds of cruising sail boats have been equipped with this rig and it has proven to be a viable alternative to the more popular traditional and modern rigs.

Modern junk rigs are capable of creditable windward performance and can often out-reach and out-run boats fitted with more conventional sail plans. Some of the advantages of the junk rig are easy reefing, low initial and maintenance costs, lack of standing rigging (less to go wrong), and a certain beauty.

BOWSPRITS

One item that is not out of place with any rig is a bowsprit and many modern Bermudan cruising rigs, as well as traditional boats, sport this appendage. Some are short affairs used simply to keep the anchor out of the way and to provide a platform ahead of the forestay, thus making it easier to handle the larger headsails. If, due to change in trim through loading, bad design or for some other reason your boat develops excessive weather helm, then the presence of a bowsprit will most likely help to solve the problem. For instance if your problem is excessive weather helm, then moving the forestay forward may be all that is required to improve the situation. Weather helm can be caused by many factors and is sometimes a combination of several design faults. Shifting the centre of effort of the sailplan forward can often solve the problem. Adding a bowsprit is usually easier that moving the mast and rigging or other drastic alterations such as reshaping underwater sections of the hull.

The type of bowsprit I prefer is one built of 1½ in to 3 in (35 mm – 75 mm) galvanised or stainless steel pipe bent round in a open U shape and then decked in teak. This arrangement is strong and provides a generous working area forward of the bow. If you are not used to this type of appendage you will soon learn to allow for its length when docking or

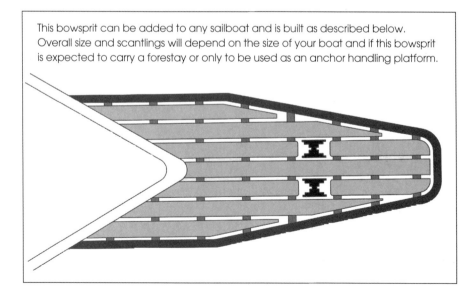

This bowsprit can be added to any sailboat and is built as described below. Overall size and scantlings will depend on the size of your boat and if this bowsprit is expected to carry a forestay or only to be used as an anchor handling platform.

Hand-sized and/or spliced rigging can save you money and looks fine on the more traditional cruising sailboats.

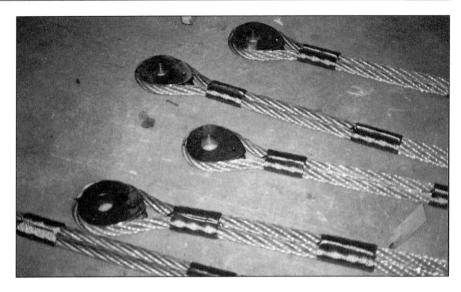

making other manoeuvres at close quarters. The bowsprit is more of a help than a hindrance and is most useful when picking up moorings, handling the anchor and dealing with unruly headsails. Depending on the length of your bowsprit, you may require a bobstay.

Many 'performance cruisers' incorporate carbon fibre pole bowsprits. These are usually of variable length and used to set the cruising spinnaker. This pole arrangement is not new, we used similar timber poles in the early 1960s and called the sails 'ballooners' or 'cruising chutes' plus a few other names if they got out of control! Personally I do not believe the symmetrical regular spinnaker has any place on a cruising boat but the asymmetrical cruising spinnaker is well worth consideration and especially if you have a reasonably active crew.

STANDING RIGGING

Many of the used production boats you may consider purchasing will have rigs that are worn out or totally unsuitable for deep water cruising. Stainless steel standing rigging has a definite life span and if it is more than five years old it will need careful checking and possible replacement. All sailboats with the exception of free standing rigs will require standing rigging. Some experienced cruising people still prefer to sail with a well set up traditional rig consisting of galvanised plough steel stays and shrouds all hand spliced and prepared in the traditional manner.

Dyform 316 stainless steel 1 x 19 standing rigging wire is a relatively new product and was developed in 1986 to offer an alternative to rod rigging. Dyform is over 25 per cent stronger and has 30 per cent less stretch than similar sized regular stainless rigging. Early versions of this wire had some minor problems, mainly some sharp edges and minor rusting due to too low a polish, however these deficiencies have long since been remedied, and this rigging wire is now widely accepted by those

Wire Diameter	Dyform wire		Conventional wire		Rod		Equivalent rod
	Break (316) lbs	Weight lbs/100 ft	Break (316) lbs	Weight lbs/100 ft	Break (316) lbs	Weight lbs/100 ft	
$3/16$	4,928	8.5	3,960	7.10	5,000	8.7	-4
5 mm	5,368	9.0	4,400	8.20	6,000	10.1	-6
6 mm	7,810	13.0	6.336	11.80	NA	NA .	NA
$1/4$	8,844	14.8	7,084	13.00	8,600	14.8	-8
$9/32$	10,802	17.4	7,810	16.10	9,900	17.5	-10
$5/16$	13,530	23.2	10,208	21.00	11,800	20.1	-12
$3/8$	19,272	32.7	14,476	29.00	17,650	30.2	-17
10 mm	21,494	36.3	15,950	32.80	NA	NA	NA
11 mm/ $7/16$	26,620	45.7	19,294	39.70	21,500	37.6	-22
12 mm	31,746	54.0	22,880	47.50	NA	NA	NA
$1/2$	34,833	59.5	25,630	53.30	30,000	52.4	-30
14 mm/ $9/16$	42,460	77.0	31,196	64.30	36,000	67.4	-40
16 mm/ $5/8$	56,320	99.0	40,832	84.00	46,000	84.4	-48
19 mm/ $3/4$	70,400	138.0	47,564	118.00	59,000	117.00	-60
$7/8$	–	–	63,964	222.00	65,000	136.00	-66

STRENGTH/WEIGHT COMPARISONS

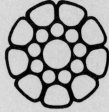

Dyform 1 x 19 is an alternative to rod rigging

cruising people who have made a study of the various types of rigging wire. Dyform can be swaged or it makes a perfect companion to Norseman end fittings.

No matter what type of rig you select or what type of materials you choose, remember that if you can fix it yourself you will be much happier than if you require outside assistance every time something goes wrong. It is obvious that help is not available in the middle of the ocean; it is equally undesirable if you have to pay some 'expert' to bring your boat up to operating condition every time you make port.

Unless you have a paid crew, you had better learn how to fix almost everything on your cruising boat. You cannot fix machine-made splices, but you can change Norseman, Sta-Lock or similar end fittings; if you have a traditional rig, you should be able to splice up new rigging as required.

When I came into yachting in the early sixties it was about the time that

Norseman terminals come in all sizes including this monster which was one of many used on the Mexican 300 ft (91.4 m) training barque *Cuauhtemoc.*

boat owners were making the transition from running rigging made from natural materials to synthetics. Having experienced both, I along with most other cruising sailors prefer the artificial variety which is generally less bulky, more reliable, lasts longer and is easier to handle. No matter if your cordage is natural fibre or synthetic, make sure you know how to splice and care for all the lines on your boat and always carry adequate spare line.

MASTS AND SPARS

With the development of modern mast building techniques in both aluminium and carbon fibre spars, the whole matter as to what type of rig and number of masts needs more careful consideration. The return in popularity of the gaff rig for traditional and some not so traditional boats, the acceptance of free standing rigs used in conjunction with both modern and traditional arrangements such as the lug or Chinese junk sail plans, means you must give considerable thought to the best choice of rig for your boat.

You may think that this is all academic if you intend to purchase a used or a new vessel. However, many older boats will need so much gear renewed that it may be worth considering replacing the entire rig. You may be able to improve and update the rig by having the new one designed around the existing mast and chainplate location. In any case if you are planning to renew, replace or redesign the rig you will need the assistance of a person qualified to advise you in this area. If you are able to make contact with the original designer of the boat then this is your best option, otherwise engage a competent naval architect or yacht designer to help you with your new sail plan and rig replacement.

The loads on masts have not changed, they must still withstand compression (downward thrust) torsion (twisting from the spreaders) and local loads from boom, spinnaker pole and boom vang. Current thinking is that weight is more important than windage so it is important to choose a mast of adequate stiffness and strength while keeping the weights within reasonable limits. This is where the more recent developments in mast technology come into play. For instance in a typical 50 ft (15 m) boat, a retro-fit from an overweight older aluminium spar to a modern one made of the same material, can save considerable weight aloft. It is well to remember that because of the difference in distance from the centre of gravity, each single unit of weight saved aloft is worth several units of ballast.

In the 1960s the teardrop shape with a constant wall thickness was thought to give the best strength for weight ratio in most aluminium extruded spars. The 1970s saw the development of the elliptical section which has now evolved to the almost squarish section that represents the latest thinking in this area. It has been proven that the further the side walls of the mast are located from the neutral axis (the centre of the mast in sectional view) the stiffer the spar. In stayed rigs, round sections are the least efficient and squarish sections are the most efficient because they locate more wall material farther from the neutral axis.

Plate masts

Rolled plate masts (as opposed to extruded sections) are becoming more popular for larger boats. The advantages of this construction include the fact that plate aluminium is stronger than extruded sections, therefore the wall thickness can be thinner for any given strength; the higher up the mast, the less need for strength. The wall thickness may be reduced towards the top of the mast, the result being weight-saving where it is most beneficial. Plate masts can more easily be tapered from the mast heel to masthead, enabling more weight-saving and adding aesthetic appeal to the mast. The benefits of this mast construction result in a lower centre of gravity.

Carbon fibre masts

Carbon fibre is now widely used in the marine industry and it is worth considering this material for your new or renewed cruising rig. This type of mast was originally used exclusively in conjunction with unstayed rigs and early examples were the subject of breakages. The failures of some of the early carbon fibre spars could be partly due to the fact that a new material (carbon fibre) was partnered with new rig technology (unstayed masts) so the experience gained in both areas makes it worth having another look at carbon.

Another problem with carbon has been its high cost, usually about double that of an aluminium spar of equal strength. This higher cost is somewhat offset by the fact that most of the rigging is not required when the material is used in an unstayed rig. Carbon fibre fatigue properties are superior to aluminium meaning that in a mast it can flex more, and more frequently without failure. A carbon fibre mast weighs only 50 per cent to 60 per cent of an aluminium spar of equal strength and stiffness; this is another benefit, especially when considering ballast requirements. The boat's ballast, the carrying capacity of stores and water, are all factors that are interrelated, when choosing a new rig. The choice of carbon fibre is not limited to free standing rigs; already a few owners of conventionally rigged, performance-oriented cruising boats have chosen this material for their spars. One drawback to using a carbon fibre mast is that you will need to make special provision against lightning striking your mast (see details in chapter 11).

Mast steps

No matter whether your mast is deck stepped or keel stepped it will need some form of step to secure the lower end of the spar. Many commercially manufactured masts come complete with a cast aluminium step that is fastened to the deck and the mast simply sits in this arrangement. Check that your deck-mounted mast step has the ability to drain water that lodges around the bottom of the mast. A tabernacle mast step may also be considered if your mast is not too long or too large; check with the designer of your particular boat regarding this option. Examine a mast support post that may be 3 in (75 mm) or larger diameter metal pipe to ensure that it is up to the job. Your mast support underneath the deck may be in the form of a beefed-up bulkhead; look for stress cracks and other tell-tale signs to show if the bulkhead needs strengthening.

If your mast is stepped on the keel, check if you have an arrangement that will allow you to alter the rake of the mast (this will change the fore-and-aft location of the foot of the mast).

Steps on the mast

Wherever possible you should fit the main mast with a set of steps for going aloft. Steps combined with a safety line are much safer than using a bosun's chair. The steps should have flat treads about 2 in (50 mm) wide as all pipe treads are murder on bare feet. Steps should be carefully laid out and you can incorporate the spreaders into the system. Make sure that the step after the spreader follows your natural climbing pattern and that you do not have to change feet as you proceed aloft.

For gaff-rigged boats where mast hoops or a similar arrangement precludes the use of mast steps, then ratlines are a good alternative. Although they usually do not continue up as high as mast steps, they have a superior appearance on any traditionally rigged cruising boat.

Deck lights

No matter what type of mast you select make sure you have adequate deck lighting; these lights are usually located on the spreaders so they will need to be considered at the same time as the mast. The masts on larger cruising boats are required to carry a selection of equipment including radar, radio aerials, communication domes, as well as a variety of lights; keep this in mind when selecting the mast(s) for your cruising boat.

WINCHES

The first cruising boat I ever sailed on had no winches. Dougie Drouin loved to do things the traditional way and his 35 ft (10.7 m) timber boat reflected his belief that sailing was a sport and as such, one was meant to extend oneself. But he did make generous use of tackles and purchases to raise and handle the sails, break out the anchor and every other activity where additional strength was required. Today I do not think any crew would stay around for long on a boat as basically equipped as this.

When it comes to selecting winches it is much better to select a few well-made and powerful examples than to cover your boat with several that will barely do the job. Today self-tailing winches are considered the norm. Thoughtful layout of the running rigging can allow one winch to serve more than one line or even one purpose. Winches need to be well fastened and the mounting area reinforced as necessary to provide a strong point capable of spreading the load and accepting the enormous forces generated when a winch is used to its full potential.

CLEATS AND FAIRLEADS

Make sure your cleats are an adequate size to handle the lines intended for them: they may be made of aluminium, stainless steel or hardwood. Try to position them in such a way as to minimise the chances of stubbing your toe. In many cases cleats have to be where they have to be, but you can usually manage to avoid locating them in the most dangerous places. Fastening the cleats to decks, coamings and cabin tops takes the same care as is used to install the winches.

For anchoring mooring lines to the hull I prefer 'bitts' to cleats; the bitt usually consists of two vertical posts with a cross bar to tie off the line. In the case of steel decks, it is possible to weld cleats and bitts directly to the deck. When securing to glassfibre or timber decks make sure that the bolts used to anchor these items to the deck are backed up with pads and large washers.

You will often need to install fairleads to avoid sheets and other lines fouling part of the rigging, coamings or other items of the superstructure. These and similar items need to be well attached and preferably installed in such a location and manner so as to not provide a hazard for the crew when moving about the decks.

When you are choosing blocks there is no need to purchase the latest 'high tech' gear. Good solid quality blocks will serve you well. Make sure you carefully match the line to the correct sheave size and that all sheet leads are arranged so that your blocks are allowed to do their work without undue strain caused by poorly laid out sheeting. You may need turning blocks and other similar arrangements to avoid chafing your lines.

SAILS

The standard way to describe the dimensions of sails is as follows:

P = The length of the luff (the edge that is attached to the mast) of the mainsail or mizzen.

E = The length of the foot (the edge that is normally attached to the boom) of the mainsail or mizzen.

J = The distance from the front of the mast to the forestay.

I = The height of the jib halyard from the deck, in the case of masthead rig this will generally be the height of the mast from the deck.

For cruising sails you should still choose Dacron which offers the best all round performance and serviceability. The variety of materials used in building sails for the racing fraternity is best left alone and even if you can afford these materials, you will find that repairs and general servicing of the sails is far more difficult than with a normal Dacron sail.

All cruising sails should be triple stitched and particular attention should be paid to the leather and other hand work required to finish off a good cruising sail. You should consider the ultraviolet resistance of the various types of sail 'cloth' before ordering. On all but the smallest boats you should carry a sewing machine capable of making repairs to your sails and other 'canvas work' on your boat. Needless to say you should also carry a full set of sail-making tools including a palm, needles and thread. I have known many cruising people who have made their own sails, some from kits, others have cut and sewn their complete sail wardrobe from scratch. Making even one sail will give you a better understanding of the techniques required to make repairs when these become necessary.

REEFING ARRANGEMENTS

When considering your sail plan, an early decision will be needed as to how to reef. For the mainsail 'jiffy' reefing is the simplest and likely to give you the least problems. Most mainsails will accept three rows of reef points and a variety of arrangements can be used to secure these to the boom; permanently installed reef pennants look fine on traditional rigs.

Roller furling in the mast is a popular option, however when the sail is reefed you still have the weight of a large portion of the sail high above the deck. Another arrangement is where the sail is furled on a spar attached to the aft face of the mast. In my opinion, boom roller reefing makes more sense and is a modern development of the earlier arrangement where we had a handle on the fore side of the mast and a bolt through to the boom. We reefed the mainsail by rolling it around the outside of the boom. The modern equivalent of boom mainsail reefing involves having the sail roll up inside the boom. To date this arrangement is only limited by the size of boom needed to contain the rolled up sail; more sophisticated arrangements are allowing boats with larger mainsails to have in-boom furling; check with your spar supplier for latest developments.

For the headsails you may wish to consider roller furling. If your cruising is mostly coastal then roller furling has a lot to recommend it. The convenience of being able to reef the headsail from the security of the cockpit will appeal to most members of the family crew. I do not like this arrangement for serious offshore work. Roller furling jibs are notorious for unfurling at the wrong moment and on many occasions the headsail has to be cut down to get it under control. This arrangement also leaves the weight of the sail aloft when it would be better stowed below.

Those who are considering roller furling units should make sure that they have strong well constructed bearings at both the top and bottom of the unit. The bearings should be well made and built from stainless steel. Check that the luff extrusion is large enough to do the job; the small elliptically shaped ones are best avoided. Instead look for a heavy duty round section that can stand up to the rigours of cruising. Check the upper bearing will not foul the mast or become entangled with the halyard.

If you are have a roller furling headsail then it is essential that you have a back-up additional forestay to support your mast in the event of the headsail arrangement failing. There have been several reported cases where the head-stay has broken below the roller furling drum. This extra stay may be needed to set a storm jib or other headsail in the event that this action is required. Again this is a choice that should be tempered by where and under what conditions you plan to be cruising. When you know that assistance or the safety of a secure harbour will always be within a short distance your choices may be different to those you would make when you are planning long-distance offshore voyaging. It is possible to have reef points in a headsail; one does not often see this arrangement but it does work especially when combined with a self-tending foresail.

STORM SAILS AND SPINNAKERS

Storm sails very seldom appear on modern sail plans, but if you are planning long offshore passages there may be a good case for including these items in your sail wardrobe. Dedicated storm sails usually consist of a heavily constructed and reinforced storm jib and trysail. Special sheeting

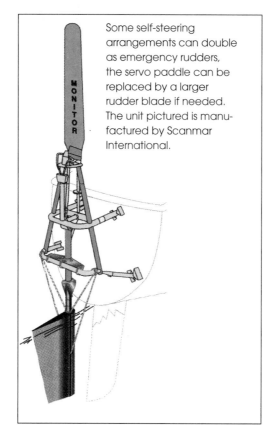

Some self-steering arrangements can double as emergency rudders, the servo paddle can be replaced by a larger rudder blade if needed. The unit pictured is manufactured by Scanmar International.

arrangements will have to be provided for both items as the sheets normally lead to a different deck location than the regular sails.

Spinnakers have frequently been in and out of fashion as a cruising boat accessory. The development of the 'gennicker' or 'cruising shute' does make this item worth considering if you have a reasonably active crew (including yourself) and you like to get every ounce of performance out of your boat. Regular spinnakers are another matter, in my opinion they have no place aboard any offshore cruising boat; if you doubt my word, look at the more dramatic photos in the racing sailing magazines or coffee table yachting books.

SELF-STEERING

Your cruising boat's self-steering ability often depends on starting with a well balanced hull and there have been many examples where the hull made a major contribution to this desirable feature. The *Spray* is one of the best known vessels with a reputation for self-steering ability. With most modern and many traditional designs the sail plan will play a big part in keeping the boat on track; it is worth keeping this in mind when deciding on your sail plan and reefing arrangements.

Self-steering wind vanes usually work well with most rigs. A visit to any major boatshow will confirm that there are almost as many self-steering devices available as there are hull types. Most of these arrangements work well and you will need to study the performance characteristics and construction detail as well before making a selection. More recently one sees more boats fitted with electronic self-steering devices as manufactured by Autohelm, Navico and Cetrek. No matter how effective these wind or electrically driven self-steering aids perform, there is no substitute for a well balanced hull and rig combination (see Appendix 3).

CHAPTER 5

Interiors

If you choose to purchase a ready-built boat then you will have limited choice when it comes to arranging your accommodation. There is not much sense in buying a boat where the interior is complete and then proceed to tear it apart. If the price of your acquisition reflects the fact that you are going to 'redo' the entire accommodation then you will be in a similar position to someone fitting out a new custom boat. If you are buying a new boat or renewing the interior, below decks is one area where you should consult your partner right from the beginning.

HOW MANY WILL IT SLEEP?

When enquiring about a particular boat, many people ask 'how many will it sleep?' Although this is a serious question it should not be the overriding consideration. 'How many will it live?' Although ungrammatical, this would be a more sensible enquiry.

Make sure your cruising boat is set up for the *least* number of people you intend to have occupying the boat long term. Sometimes one is tempted to treat boats like houses; you may not need a four-bedroom home other than for the resale value. Resale value of a boat is very important but the number of berths alone will never sell a boat to a knowledgeable person. As you are setting up your boat for cruising, your most likely buyer will be someone who wants to use the boat for the same purpose. If too many berths are included at the expense of other items then you will not only have suffered the inconvenience of a less than perfect layout, but you will find your boat difficult to sell when you are ready to move on.

The most likely numbers of crew for a cruising boat are the two owners with either two children or another couple as occasional crew or as charterers. If you think you are likely to want to sleep a total of six occasionally, then the lounge or dinette can easily be arranged to sleep the extra two as required. So we now have the perfect cruising boat that sleeps two in luxury, two in some comfort and two on a temporary basis.

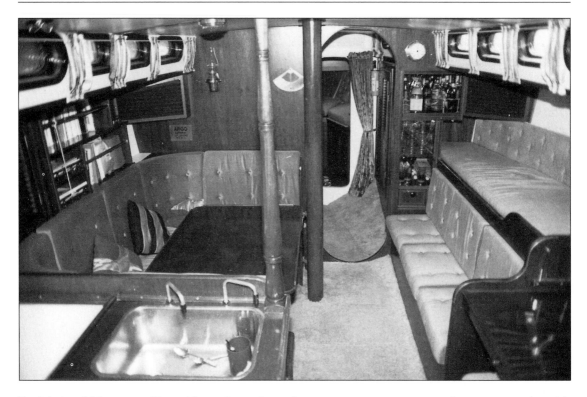

The interior of this steel New Zealand-built 38 ft (11.6 m) sailboat illustrates a simple but functional use of space.

Even if you intend to charter to one or two couples or a couple with two children, you can then give up your own accommodation to the paying passengers and use the dinette or other convertible accommodation for yourselves. You will almost certainly be last to bed and first to rise so this arrangement will work better than you might think.

To give an example of my own arrangements, our boat K*I*S*S, a Spray 28, had a comfortable double cabin in the bow and a make-up double or single in the pilot house. The settees were too short to sleep anyone other than the smallest child. Naturally my wife Gwenda and I used the forward cabin. However, we found that when we had visitors it was easier for us (last to bed/first to rise) to give the guests the forward cabin and use the pilot house berths for ourselves. Our current boat is 38 ft (11.6 m) and although it is much more luxurious, we deliberately chose a similar layout and stuck to the same sleeping arrangements.

For offshore cruising you will probably require at least two single berths that are located in a part of the vessel with the least motion. These 'sea berths' should be fitted with lee cloths and designed to accommodate the off-watch crew in maximum comfort and should, if possible, not be adjacent to the high traffic areas such as the galley, chart table or the heads. Unfortunately this perfect recipe for seclusion and comfort when off watch is not possible on most cruising boats. For sleeping in port, a double berth is the ultimate for most couples. Adding the convertible dinette rounds out the full complement of sleeping accommodation.

All that I have said in the previous paragraphs applies to boats between

35 ft (10.7 m) and 45 ft (13.7 m) LOA. Cruising boats *under* 35 ft (10.7 m) are best arranged with only two permanent berths. How much additional length should one need to add permanent accommodation for two? Many clients, when discussing a new design, request us 'to just add another 7 ft (2 m) and fit in two more berths'. Not a sensible option. Those two extra people need s-p-a-c-e; they have to be fed; more stores and water will be needed plus a little more galley space; additional users will put more strain on existing showers and toilets or create the need for a second facility; a larger dining area will be required if they do not want to have to eat alone (and I have yet to sail on a boat where two sittings were considered the norm); and their gear has to be stowed. Finally, the whole crew needs room to move *and* lounge about in comfort.

For the weekend cruiser there are many compromises that are not available to the long-distance sailor. Four berths in a 25 ft (7.6 m) to 28 ft (8.5 m) sailboat can be acceptable for a few days cruising where you are a family or

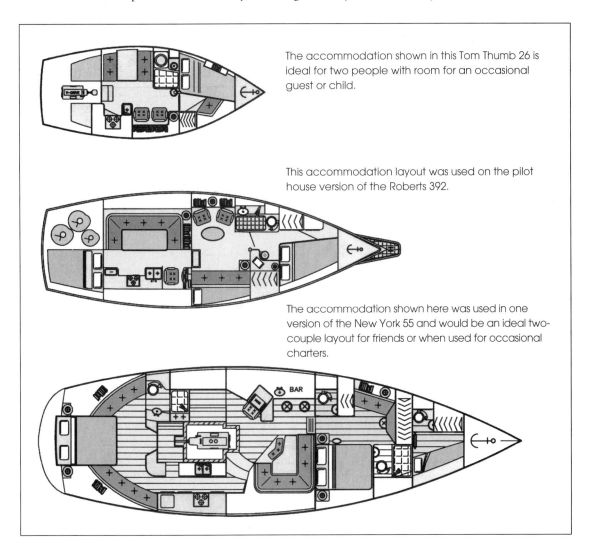

The accommodation shown in this Tom Thumb 26 is ideal for two people with room for an occasional guest or child.

This accommodation layout was used on the pilot house version of the Roberts 392.

The accommodation shown here was used in one version of the New York 55 and would be an ideal two-couple layout for friends or when used for occasional charters.

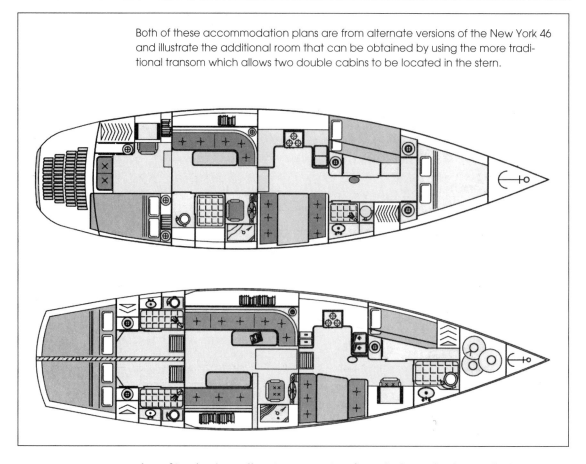

Both of these accommodation plans are from alternate versions of the New York 46 and illustrate the additional room that can be obtained by using the more traditional transom which allows two double cabins to be located in the stern.

close friends. A smaller size range is often all that a budget will allow, especially for couples with a young family. If you want to retain the interest and co-operation of your mate and the family then you may be wise to choose a boat that is less performance-oriented and which offers more living space.

Boats grow in interior space in at least two directions when length is added, so we can say that the two additional berths require another 10 ft (3 m) resulting in a boat of around 55 ft (16.7 m) LOD. Boats with different waterline lengths and different beam ratios can change the exact overall length requirement, however in general, if you intend to accommodate additional crew whether they be family or friends and especially if they are paying guests, then you should decide on your absolute needs before settling on the length, or to be more accurate the size, of your cruising boat.

HOW MANY HEADS?

After you have decided on the number of berths, the next decision is how many heads are required. This is very important area of your boat and some time should be taken in considering the available options, especially if your boat is intended as a live-aboard long-distance cruiser. In boats without a dedicated shower stall, a low usage portable shower head attached to a flexible pipe can be led up through the back of the basin and do double duty as a basin tap and shower head. In boats with an LOA of around 25 ft (7.6 m) to say 36 ft (11 m), a single head with toilet, hand basin and shower is the norm. Once boats reach 37 ft (11.3 m) then many owners start to consider two separate heads. In my opinion, boats under 43 ft (13.1 m) are better arranged with a single complete head and shower facility. A good compromise is to have a separate shower stall; in practice this arrangement has proven to work out well as it allows two people to use the separate facilities at the same time.

If your boat is over 43 ft (13 m) then you may wish to consider two separate heads complete with showers. It is a good idea to have two toilets if your *regular* crew totals four and essential if there are more than this number aboard regularly. To sum up I suggest you consider the following options depending on the space available and the number of crew: one roomy head complete with shower; one head with separate shower stall; two toilet compartments, one with a separate shower stall; two complete head and shower compartments.

CABIN SOLES

When constructing a boat most builders install the soles (floor of the cabin) before fitting the furniture and joinery. A highly-polished teak and holly sole is a glorious thing (alternate strips of 1½ in (35 mm) teak and ¼ in (12 mm) holly which is a white timber), but not on a cruising boat. These polished areas are far too slippery. In rough conditions you will have enough trouble staying upright on even the best non-skid surface.

It is best if the sole can be the same level throughout the boat; this avoids one area where one can trip when moving about the vessel, however in the real world this is seldom practical and if you have a pilot house it is impossible. Make sure any changes in sole level are really necessary; raising the sole in the area of the dinette may be worthwhile to allow the occupants to see out while seated.

Lowering the sole where it is necessary to gain proper headroom is another valid reason and if your boat has a centre cockpit and you can fit in a walk-through then you may find the sole has to be lowered in the passageway to make best use of the available space under and beside the cockpit.

Plywood will almost certainly be the basic building material used to construct the sole of your boat. Now the question is where do we go from there. Probably the least expensive and best non-skid solution would be to paint the sole with deck paint; not very glamorous but very practical at sea. For serious long-distance cruising you may have a plywood sole, and then choose a varnish that offers some non-skid qualities and this sole could have loose mat covers for use when in port. My personal choice is to have a plywood sole and then install fitted carpet that can easily be taken up and dried as required. Let's face it; the area of carpet is so small that you could replace it every few months and still not be sent to the poor house.

The interior of any cruising boat should reflect the owner's personality; the light interior of *Lucia* is the perfect match for single-hander Maureen Jenkins. *Photo: Paul Fay*

Before you add any covering to the sole you will need to decide if any storage lockers will be located in the bilge. You should carefully cut openings in these areas, saving the cut-outs for use as lids. Another suggestion is to arrange the cut-outs as receptacles for rectangular plastic bins; these are especially useful in the galley area where you may have the space under the sole to accommodate the bins. The plastic bins are available from supermarkets and service stations and come in a variety of sizes. For a superior finish the access locker tops are carpeted and the tops and aperture are edged in flat aluminium trim. A stainless steel ring pull completes the arrangement.

LOCKERS AND SHELVING

As mentioned earlier there will be many areas under the sole where you are able to arrange additional stowage lockers; this area is ideally suited for stowage of those items you wish to keep cool.

Under the berths you can arrange lockers in the outward facing areas plus additional stowage accessed through the top of the berth; the latter is most suitable for stowing items that may be bulky and/or less often required. Often it will be possible to arrange lockers or shelving above, and outboard, of the berths, the choice will depend on the space available in the particular area. When arranging lockers and shelves remember that it is always wise to stow heavier items as low in the boat as is practical. The first rough weather you encounter will surely concentrate your mind when it comes to good and bad stowage practices. The saying 'a place for everything and everything in its place' must surely have been coined by a sailor.

Unless you have a very large boat you should keep hanging lockers to a minimum. Over the 30 years that I have been designing cruising boats I have seen the 'dress code' of the general population change from a standard where every occasion required a set form of dress to the modern norm where almost anything can be worn at any event. These changes along with easy-care fabrics used in modern clothing make the hanging locker almost obsolete. A 'wet locker' is still a necessity; if this can be arranged adjacent to the engine room or other area where heat is generated then the wet to dry process will be suitably accelerated.

A well thought out boat will have numerous spaces where lockers and shelves are installed; a careful assessment of your boat may reveal additional possibilities in areas overlooked by the designer or builder.

Sail locker

We should include a sizeable sail locker in any cruising sail boat. This item has shrunk in size over the years because when not in use mainsails are usually covered and left on the boom, where roller furling is fitted, sails are left up for months on end. Other jibs are often stowed flaked down and roped to the pulpit. Only the extras such as cruising spinnakers, storm sails and the like are stowed below; hence the smaller sail lockers. All of this is bad news for the longevity of the sails; if the sails that are left on deck do not get washed overboard, then unnecessary exposure to the sun will greatly shorten their life.

Anchor lockers which are sometimes adjacent to the sail locker are discussed in Chapter 10.

HANDHOLDS AND CORNERS

Check around the interior of your boat and see if you have a satisfactory number of grab points; the larger the interior spaces the more important it is to have grab points to hand. Vertical posts not only help to support the cabin top, they are great for using as handholds as you move about the boat in a seaway; you may find it useful to add one or two of these to an existing boat.

Check for sharp corners; our previous boat K*I*S*S had many of these bruise-causing features. My wife Gwenda commented on these corners to the owner/builder Hal Stufft. Hal told me he delayed launching his new boat because his wife Dorothy insisted that he change the interior to incorporate 'Gwenda corners' thus eliminating the problem on his new boat.

THE GALLEY

The galley is an area that needs careful consideration. It should be practical as 'keeping the cook happy' goes a long way to a providing a congenial atmosphere aboard any cruising boat. The location is important and consideration should be given to placing the galley where the motion is least, adjacent to the eating area and out of the way of through traffic. The cook should have a comfortable working environment and he or she will want to

On centre-cockpit boats the galley is often located in the 'walk-through' area beside the cockpit; this is satisfactory provided the 'chef' is not too isolated from the action.

be able to see out and not feel isolated from the rest of the crew and their activities. Placing the galley adjacent the companionway helps keep the cook in touch with the rest of the crew and also helps with the ventilation of the cooking smells, steam, etc. There will need to be adequate counter space and specific allocated stowage space for stores, cooking utensils and crockery.

Traditionally, the galley was placed to port, the idea being that when a vessel was on the starboard tack the galley was on the low side and provided a more comfortable position for the cook. A sailing boat has the right of way when on the starboard tack so the cook would not be disturbed by the necessity of the vessel having to tack to avoid another. In the real world it is wise to keep out of the way of any large vessel so it is practical to place the galley on either side of the hull.

Placing the galley out of the way of through traffic usually results in an L or U shaped arrangement. Either layout works well but the U shape can be better. The sides of the U usually run across the vessel and should not be more than 2 ft 6 in (762 mm) apart as this allows the cook to move around without being thrown about when the going gets rough. Suitable anchor points for a restraining sling can easily be arranged in the U shaped galley. A suitable handhold is often provided by a pole extending from the half bulkhead that divides the galley from the accommodation, to the deck head. Other handholds should be provided not only in the galley but throughout the entire cabin areas.

Needless to say there should be as many galley storage lockers as possible. There will need to be dedicated spaces for various sized plates, mugs and glasses. Do not forget to include a garbage locker; if this is on one side of the open end of the U then it can hinge outwards from the bottom. It is important to provide adequate ventilation in all lockers especially those containing perishable foods. Louvre doors, mesh grills and other devices can be used to ensure that fresh air is able to circulate freely.

Make sure that the locker doors and drawers will stay shut in a seaway. For drawers, the most often used closure method is a notch in the drawer runners so that the drawer has to be raised before sliding outwards. For locker doors the recommended method is to have a finger hole with a catch located inside and accessed through the hole. This is also widely used as a positive method of securing drawers. Push-pull, tongue and ball bearing catches are often used for locker doors, these are usually noisy to close and can come open if the contents of the locker is thrown against the door. The most attractive catch that can be used on both doors and drawers consists of a cast-brass, flush-fitting catch that fits flush with the front and has a pull-out-and-twist handle; this is the most attractive and positive solution to an age-old problem. If buying a new or used boat, examine the construction of these items and be prepared to modify them if they are not up to the job.

Stoves

The stove is usually placed at the bottom of the U so that it can be gimbled to stay level as the vessel heels; a system of rails and pot restrainers is essential. The type of fuel used to power the stove will depend on the cook's personal preference and the main choices are: gas, usually butane, or propane (in USA compressed natural gas is the optimum), paraffin (kerosene), methylated spirits (alcohol) and diesel oil. It may be possible to use electricity for cooking, but this is unusual except in the largest of cruising yachts. Microwaves are now often seen on all types of boats and many are designed to work well on 12 volt systems as well as shore power.

Each fuel has its own advantages and disadvantages. For instance, gas is clean and easy to use and probably the most popular choice at the present time. The one disadvantage of gas is that it is heavier than air and when mixed with the latter can cause violent explosions. A carefully installed gas system with safety cut-out sensors backed up by a gas detector can be a wonderful shipmate. Needless to say, the gas bottles should be in separate self-draining lockers. Although the fittings used to connect gas bottles to the system do vary in various countries, propane or butane gas is readily obtainable in most locations throughout the world. If you are cruising in an area where compressed natural gas is available then that would be my first choice as it is lighter than air and is much safer than either butane or propane.

Paraffin (kerosene) is probably the next most popular cooking stove fuel and is obtainable world-wide, however, anything but the cleanest and purest material will soon clog the burners of your stove and give you untold problems. Although there are supposedly no-odour varieties available, many people cannot stand the smell of burning paraffin. Best check with the cook before installing this type of stove. If you have a paraffin stove this will need to be preheated with methylated spirit, so that is another volatile liquid to be purchased and stored.

If the climate allows, and you have the room, then a diesel fired galley stove like this one made by Dickinson is an ideal shipmate.

At first glance it would seem that the perfect stove would be diesel-fired. I did use one of these aboard a large trading ketch and found it reliable and efficient. One problem with this type of stove is that it takes some time to reach operating temperature and consequently cannot be turned off and on like a gas stove. Once you get a diesel-fuelled stove operational it generally stays on. In hot climates the stove being continually in service is not a practical consideration so these stoves are best suited to boats operating in colder areas of the world; they can also be used to power the cabin heating and hot water systems. The main advantage of this stove is that it uses the same fuel as your diesel engine. If your boat is over 40 ft (12 m) and you plan to be cruising in the colder climes, then a diesel stove may be your choice. The Canadian-built Dickinson diesel stoves have a good reputation.

Fire extinguishers

A fire blanket is an essential item of galley equipment; this device can be most efficient in fighting the type of fire and flare up that you are likely to encounter in the galley. In addition to the fire blanket, you should have at least two fire extinguishers located in the galley area. Make sure they are of a type that is suitable for putting out the fires you are likely to encounter. The dry powder type of extinguisher is one of the most successful. A trip to your local fire station or department would be time well spent as you will learn much that may not only save your boat but your life as well. When new crew come aboard, make sure you explain the working of these items; they cannot be tested, but they can be examined and the workings explained to all.

The sink

The sink should be of reasonable proportions and, if possible, placed close to the centreline of the boat. A double sink is a nice feature if you have the space, but with a single bowl make sure is deep enough and has a decent sized draining area; a folding draining rack will be appreciated by the cook. In the past the sink was always fitted with both a salt and a fresh water pump; today's crews usually demand a less Spartan arrangement and the salt water is usually left outside the hull.

WATER TANKS

Until recently, it was necessary for the long-distance cruising boat to carry sufficient water for each leg of the voyage. This meant not only carrying large amounts of fresh water but also strict budgeting of the daily use, and in the case of a slow passage, rationing was a distinct possibility. Now that water makers are becoming less expensive, it is less essential to carry large quantities of water. An emergency, hand-operated water maker is a sensible option for even the smallest long-distance cruising boat. If your cruising is undertaken where you are able to replenish your water every few days, then you would be better off to invest in larger tanks. On medium to large boats, the making and storage of hot water can usually be arranged via the engine cooling system or by other means (see Chapter 6).

PRESSURE WATER SYSTEMS

On medium to large coastal cruising boats pressure water systems are a desirable feature. Where pressure water systems are installed in long-distance cruisers they should be so arranged that they can be switched off during passage-making legs of the voyage. This usually means a duel system of pressure water backed up by hand or foot pump arrangements on each sink and hand basin etc.

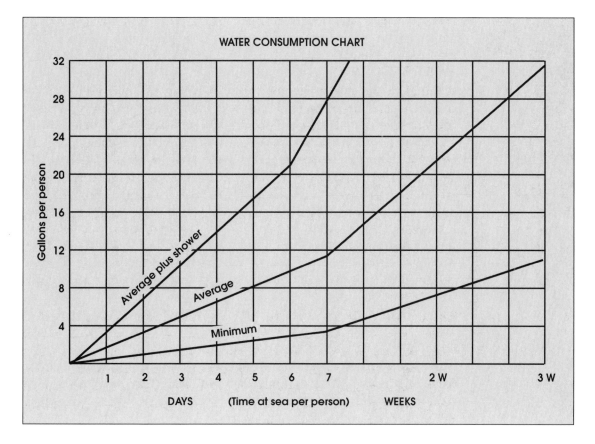

There are two basic types of pressure water systems, those with a pressure tank and those that work on demand. The former arrangement is superior because it means that pressure is maintained in a special tank and the pump does not have to operate every time a tap is turned on; the latter is annoying to those who may be sleeping when another crew member draws a drink of water.

ICE BOXES

The ice box was an essential item of any boat built before the advent of on-board refrigeration and many boats still rely on this food preservation and storage system. It is possible to produce freezing temperatures by mixing salt with crushed ice; however, the lack of a constant supply of ice usually precludes this option on your boat. If you want to be able to make ice cubes or freeze ice cream and maintain a freezer compartment on your boat then some form of mechanical refrigeration will be required. Those with smaller cruising boats who mainly undertake coastal cruising may find an ice box sufficient.

A properly built ice box should maintain temperatures at 5°–10° C right up until the ice has melted. To give some idea of what you can expect from your ice box let us consider a 2.4 cu ft (75 l) box and a 12 lb (5 kg) block of ice; this will last about two days during the summer months. As you can see this is not a practical proposition for long-distance cruising but would suffice for the weekend sailor or over the holidays in areas where replenishment of the ice is a practical alternative. If you opt for an ice box, incorporate the following features: minimum size to suit your needs, top opening, good seals, proper drainage system and most importantly at least 3 in (75 mm) of polyurethane insulation material on all faces of the box.

Many owners of coastal cruising boats rely on a portable ice box that can be brought down to a low temperature and stocked with food before leaving home.

REFRIGERATION

The refrigerator in your home is powered by a compressor which circulates the refrigerant gas through pipes which in turn force the heat out of your refrigerator cabinet. Over the past few years several systems have been developed that make it possible to transfer this and similar technology to your boat. Firstly let us consider the main practical options available to the cruising sailor.

Absorption cycle systems

These date back to the earliest refrigerators and were the first to replace the family ice box. Although now replaced in home refrigerators by efficient compressor systems, the absorption cycle system is worth serious consideration. The energy used to operate it is heat which can be supplied by burning LPG (liquified petroleum gas) or by electricity. Most of these models will run on both gas, battery supplied 12V DC or 240/120V AC mains or on-board generated electricity. Usually these units come in a ready-built cabinet and often incorporate a freezer section.

These units are best considered in situations where marina shore power is frequently available or where you have a regular supply of on-board generated AC power; they may be the perfect solution for the weekend or coastal sailor who is restricted to two or three days at sea at one time. It is not recommended to run these units on gas when the boat is under way; of course you could gimbal the whole unit but that would involve giving up considerable extra space and there are other systems more suitable for the long-distance cruiser.

Compressor driven systems

Most of these units are about the size of an under-counter bar refrigerator and have a small freezer compartment. In size and style they resemble the absorption system units. These units usually operate on 12V DC and 240 V or 120V AC. Unfortunately, unless connected to shore power or run from the on-board generating set, they will have to be run on 12V DC power and will draw an average of 5 amps from your battery. While they may be ideal for weekend sailors, they are not really a solution for the offshore passagemaker.

DC heat pumps

These operate in a similar manner to the compressor driven systems described above; their main advantage is that they are available as a separate unit that can be installed in your own purpose built compartment. These units are powered by either 12V or 24V DC battery power and have the advantage of drawing around 2 amps which is a current drain that can be sustained by most on-board electrical systems. This is one system that is worth serious consideration by those who require refrigeration and are planning extended offshore passages.

Engine driven refrigeration

This is the ultimate system for the long-distance cruiser. If you require large capacity refrigeration with freezing capabilities then one of these units will suit you best. The compressor can be belt driven off a special pulley that is either attached to the main engine or perhaps the engine that drives your generating set.

The only real drawback of these units is that they are expensive, costing over £1000 or US$1500 for the component parts; if you can install your own then this cost may be acceptable; a custom-installed unit would run the cost up to £3000 or US$4500. The engine will only need to be run about one hour per day to power this unit; if operated by the same engine as the generating set this could be a very economical and tidy arrangement to solve all your refrigeration requirements.

Other considerations

It is possible to power a small refrigeration unit with solar panel, wind generator or a combination of the two. It is worth mentioning that you will not be cruising very long before you will become involved in discussions regarding the various ways of charging your own electricity supply.

Any appliance or piece of equipment that you have aboard your boat will have to be maintained and you had better be prepared to acquire the necessary skills to keep all your equipment working. You are unlikely to be able to undertake some major repairs but you will need to take care of all the minor ones. Fortunately there are other cruising folk out there who have professional skills and who will be willing to help you out.

FURNITURE

The chart table

The chart table is an essential part of any cruising boat. In all but the smallest cruising boat it should be possible to arrange a permanent, purpose-built navigation station. A satisfactory arrangement is to use the inboard end of a quarter berth as a seat and build the chart table just ahead of this arrangement. Not only does this utilise space for two purposes (very important in any but the smallest boat) but it locates the chart table athwartships and places the navigator facing forward – the ideal arrangement. Try to incorporate space at the chart table for folded or rolled charts, electronic appliances such as radio(s), GPS and other navigational aids. Even if your boat carries mainly portable navigational equipment, it should have a regular stowage area.

Some navigators prefer to undertake their chart work standing up while others prefer to allocate any spare space to another priority and use the main saloon table for laying out the charts. You will have your own preferences, and space limitations and existing arrangements will all play their part. Given the option, unless you are prepared to have your chart work disturbed by a variety of other activities, then you will be better served with a proper navigational area, no matter how it is arranged.

The saloon table

Regarding the saloon table, here you have a myriad of choices. Many boats under 35 ft (10.7 m) are still arranged with the table more or less on the centreline and, when in use, it is impossible for any person to move forward or aft. If you can arrange the main saloon table to be off to one side of the centreline and either incorporate an L or similar arrangement for the seating, you will leave a clear space for people to move about the boat. Centreline tables were popular when boats had a much narrower beam; now we have other choices.

The saloon table is one item where you should spend considerable time studying other boats. If possible talk to other owners as everyone has their own ideas. My preference is to have the saloon table combined with an L-shaped settee and located opposite two comfortable chairs.

Settees

If your boat is already fitted out make sure that the settees and other seating are comfortable. Sometimes one can go aboard a boat where there are lots of places to sit but no comfortable seating. I like the idea of two really comfortable chairs set on one side of the cabin with a small table in between. This is the place for the captain and mate to really relax when in port or when conditions at sea permit.

Settee berths are usually just that, they are used as settees by day time and for sleeping at night. Sometimes if a settee is the correct width for seating, about 1 ft 6 in (457 mm) it is too narrow for sleeping where the correct width is about 2 ft 3 in (686 mm). This problem can be overcome at either the design or refitting stage by widening the settee and using a shaped back cushion to take up the extra width in the daytime. Hinged seat backs and other arrangements can also turn a seat into a berth.

LIGHTING

The lighting throughout your interior will need to be carefully arranged so you receive as much natural light as possible by day and economical artificial light after dark. As mentioned elsewhere, hatches with smoked or clear perspex inserts provide considerably more light than any number of portlights. Have fabric covers made for the larger hatches so on the hotter days you can keep the direct sunlight at bay. Windows and portlights do play a part in admitting light to the cabin areas, but their main function is to allow the occupants to see out.

In the modern cruising boat, the artificial lighting is mainly supplied by electricity. When you are cruising this normally means 12 volt power supplied by the domestic batteries. Small lights placed so they can be used for reading at the same time as supplying general lighting are preferred to single overhead units. Low-power, long-life bulbs are now available from the Dutch marine manufacturer, Vetus Den Ouden. Halogen lamps and fluorescent tubes are also suitable for marine use and use less power than most other types.

Nothing beats the soft light given out by a paraffin (kerosene) lamp; unfortunately it does mean carrying another fuel and the lamps can smoke and sometimes smell. Candle light is also attractive but should be restricted for use when safely tied up in a quiet berth. Any lamp or candle that emits naked flame does present an additional hazard. One has to be careful to keep this type of light well away from the deckhead as the heat directed up the glass chimney of a paraffin lamp can ignite the deckhead covering. A protective hood installed above the lamp is essential.

HATCHES AND VENTILATORS

Adequate ventilation is essential in any boat. The arrangement has to be capable of letting air flow through the boat while not admitting water at the same time. Because opening portlights are often a constant source of leaks, you should look elsewhere when planning the air flow through your interior.

Deck hatches and ventilators are the prime source of fresh air. It is not just a matter of opening the hatches on a hot day; the correct airflow has to be established to achieve the desired result. When you are sailing you will want to be able to establish an efficient airflow without admitting spray; fortunately there are a number of ways to achieve this. There are several different styles of hatch available that can be opened in more than one direction. If you have a cabin heating stove then make sure your ventilation does not interfere with its operation.

Fabric wind-scoops that can be rigged at any of your hatches are a good way of getting the air moving in the direction you desire. Dorade, mushroom and similar vents can be made and installed in such a way as to allow air in and keep water out. One or two small 12 volt fans will also work wonders in moving air throughout the interior of your boat.

HEATING

You will need an efficient heating system unless you plan to cruise exclusively in warmer climates. If you plan to live aboard permanently, then you should plan for some form of heating, no matter where you intend to cruise. My first choice, and the simplest form of heater, is a drip-fed diesel heating stove which has the advantage of using readily available fuel and providing the most heat for the least cost. One heater should be sufficient in boats up to 35 ft (10.7 m); another reason for a simple aft cockpit layout in this size of boat. This type of heater needs to be vented outside by way of a chimney. If the stove is located near a bulkhead or other joinery then that area will need insulating against the heat radiated from the stove. I have found that a stainless steel chimney known as a 'Charlie Noble', that can be taken off and stored when not in use, makes an excellent companion to a diesel heating stove. The chimney opening will require an alternative cover when the stove is not is use.

A popular heater in Europe and more recently in the US is the Eberspacher (other similar makes are also becoming available) which is a diesel-powered unit that heats the air before it is fan-driven to various vents around the boat; in effect this is a thermostatically controlled central heating system. Providing you keep it operating this is a wonderful unit, however, being somewhat complex in nature, and involving additional electrical wiring, it can only be recommended for boats around 40 ft (12 m) and larger.

Solid fuel stoves may be found on many traditional boats where they seem in keeping with the rest of the boat; however, you may have a problem stowing sufficient fuel onboard for all but the shortest of cruises. Calor or butane (LPG) gas heaters are another possibility, but following my own advice of having the minimum gas appliances aboard, I would prefer another alternative.

In most areas, the use of heaters and even the heat from the crew will cause condensation which has to be dealt with, otherwise it will be as much of a problem as allowing spray to continually invade your living area. In a larger boat you may be able to afford the luxury of a small Dri-Boy dehumidifier which will remove up to 2½ gallons (11 litres) of water per day; this water can be used in your

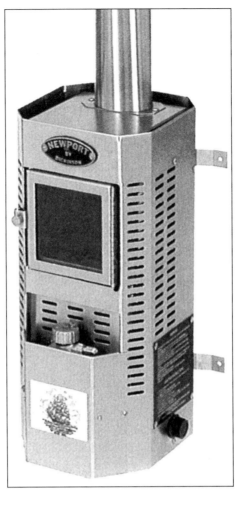

There are many efficient diesel-fuelled heating stoves available including this Dickinson Newport bulkhead mounted heater. On the right boat they can provide all the heat you could ever need.

battery. Unfortunately this is rather an expensive way of producing water to top up the battery! You can purchase bags of crystals that are specially formulated for collecting and removing moisture from the surrounding air; these are most useful to remove condensation from the air when your boat is laid up over the winter.

Some of the systems we have discussed in this chapter are not suitable for boats that are intended for serious offshore use. You will need to decide if you are capable and prepared to service and maintain complex equipment that is operating in an unfriendly environment. As a general rule, the smaller the boat, the simpler the equipment should be.

If your cruising takes you far offshore then you will need spares for every item that is repairable. Unfortunately many items, especially those of the electronic variety are not repairable, at least not repairable by most of us. Even if we are proud of our DIY skills there are limitations to our knowledge and capabilities; keep this in mind when selecting any item that is not absolutely necessary for operating your boat.

CHAPTER 6

Engines, Cooling and Fuel Systems

◆ *Propellers* ◆ *Horsepower requirements* ◆ *Engine compartments* ◆ *The engine 'drive chain'* ◆ *Stern bearings* ◆ *Ventilation* ◆ *Cooling systems* ◆ *Sail drives and outboard motors* ◆ *The instrument panel* ◆ *Fuel tanks* ◆ *Fuel and oil filters* ◆ *Micro-organisms: 'fuel bugs'*

The first engine item to consider is the auxiliary engine. Almost every boat has one, that is except for those owned by a few masochists and many of these finally give in and install some form of engine power. By engine power I mean diesel; in my opinion petrol or gasoline engines have no place in any cruising sailing boat, or in any other boat for that matter.

Some clients ask their naval architect to produce a design that will give maximum performance under both sail and power. This is difficult to achieve; not only difficult but expensive. To keep a sail boat performing at its best under all conditions one needs to minimise the non-contributing projections below the waterline; naturally this includes the propeller. To drive any vessel at its best speed requires a propeller that is matched to the correct power. As you can see there is already some conflict between these two requirements.

TYPES OF PROPELLERS

The most efficient propeller from a sailing point of view (excluding none at all) is the two-blade folding variety. The two blades mean a larger diameter and this can cause problems where space is restricted. Some of these two-bladed folding jobs are notoriously inefficient and others have a reputation for not always opening on demand, which could be disastrous. If you opt for this type, make sure you are able to get a first-hand recommendation from someone who has already had favourable experience with a particular brand.

There are ways around the problem, for example using feathering propellers, but these are complex and expensive. Remember the KISS principle; finely engineered feathering propellers may be suitable for larger yachts where the owners have the resources to cover the initial expense and possible high maintenance costs. But unless you have a very deep pocket, you are best advised to accept a small loss of speed under sail and select a three-bladed prop with the correct diameter and pitch for your cruising boat.

HORSEPOWER REQUIREMENTS

You will want to know whether the engine on your boat has sufficient power to do the job; usually it is too late if you make a bad decision. The auxiliary is often undervalued until the day (or more likely the dark night) when you need it most. There are many formulas used to correlate the power of the auxiliary to your boat and to ensure it is up to the task; for preliminary calculations we use a power to weight ratio. This simple calculation will tell you if your engine has enough power for your needs.

We can start with a 'ball park' calculation, and estimate that for any cruising boat, two horsepower per 1000 lb (454 kg) displacement is the minimum requirement. The addition or reduction of horsepower from the above calculation will depend on your philosophy. In general US sailors prefer more power than their European counterparts.

Almost all inboard engines fitted to sailing boats require gearing down to produce shaft rotation reduction by way of a transmission gear box. In general we usually recommend a 2:1 reduction, thus halving the rotation rate of the propeller versus the engine revolutions. You will find that most manufacturers have options in the 1.9:1 to 2.15:1 range; this falls within the 2:1 recommendation. You can gear down your engine more than usual to give *maximum performance at lower speeds* and so reduce the amount of horsepower required to drive your vessel. This option results in a larger diameter propeller and there may not be room for it; you will also have induced more drag, hence less sailing performance.

When considering 'horsepower', there are several terms used to convey the power generated by the engine at certain revolutions. Terms you will encounter include brake horsepower (BHP). This is the power put out by the engine but does not include the power loss caused by the transmission gearbox or other losses due to such items as an alternator, water pump and general friction of the transmission system. Shaft horsepower (SHP) represents the available power at the propeller.

Usually more than one rating is shown. For instance *maximum*, this is the power you could get for a very short time before you burn up the engine; *intermittent*, this is the power that the engine can deliver for the limited period usually 30 to 60 minutes; *continuous*, is the rating which the engine can operate at for long periods without damage – obviously a prime consideration. Increasingly you will find that the power ratings are given in Kw and the conversions are as follows: 1 Kw = 1.359 HP

ENGINE COMPARTMENTS

When choosing your engine you must ensure there is sufficient room to install or retro-fit your choice. It is not just a matter of shoe-horning the engine into a given space, you will need room for insulation and for servicing. If access is difficult then there is always the chance you will neglect the maintenance. Make sure you can easily reach the oil dipstick, water and oil filters and the important primary fuel filter. Can you easily obtain access to the injectors, stuffing box, water pump and impeller?

Insulation

Insulation in one form or another is essential if you want to avoid the annoyance of the noise emitted by an auxiliary engine. Modern engines make much less noise than their forebears but the modern cruising sailor is perhaps less tolerant, so proper insulation is essential.

The builder of my previous boat *K*I*S*S* fitted a replacement engine with only fractions of inches to spare so insulation was virtually non-existent. Coming from the 'old school' I did not find the noise a problem but my purchaser immediately decided to find a way to insulate the engine.

MOUNTINGS, COUPLINGS, STUFFING BOXES, WATER SEALS AND SHAFT BEARINGS

The long subheading clearly illustrates how these items are linked. You must consider the 'drive train' of your engine as a single integrated unit.

Mountings

Your auxiliary engine must have flexible mountings and a suitable coupling such as an Aqua Drive flexible unit to complete the vibration-free installation. The Aqua Drive allows for slight misalignment between the shaft and the engine transmission; this is a necessary feature because when the engine is mounted on flexible mountings there will be some movement between the engine coupling and the propeller shaft. I have seen engines mounted directly on to the engine beds, but this is not a satisfactory arrangement as the vibration, caused by the engine and transmitted to the hull, are noisy and uncomfortable; today most engines are set on flexible mountings.

Stuffing box or packing gland

You will need some form of gland to prevent the water entering your boat where the propeller shaft leaves the propeller tube. Your main choices will be between a traditional stuffing box and one of the newer sealing devices, such as a Deep Sea Seal. If you choose a stuffing box, it may have an external grease lubrication system or depend on the natural oils of the 'stuffing' and the water for its lubrication. Grease-fed stuffing boxes usually employ a remote cylinder that is packed with waterproof grease;

VETUS COMPLETE STERN ASSEMBLY

These shaft assemblies protect the environment (no grease in the water) Remanit 4418 shaft material: – 60% stronger – smaller shaft diameters. All shafts of ø 40, 45 and 50mm are always supplied with the flexible stuffing box (5) with torsion protection (6).

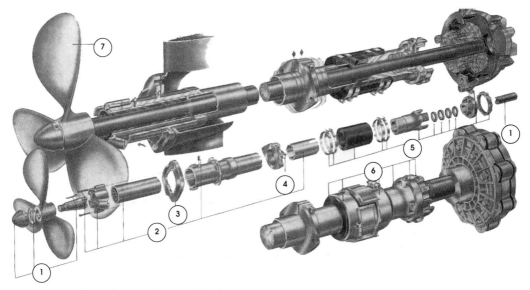

A VETUS propeller-shaft assembly consists of:

1   Tapered, straightened and polished stainless stell propeller shaft with keyway, thread, fairwatercap, lock washer and key.
2   Outer bearing (with incorporated rubber bearing) soldered to bronze stern tube.
3   Mounting flange for outer bearing.
4   Mounting flange (adjustable) for stern tube.

5   Flexible stuffing box with rubber sleeve for shaft 25, 30, 35mm diameter.
6   Flexible stuffing box with rubber sleeve and torsion protection for shaft 40, 45, 50mm diameter.
7   Propeller.

one or two turns on the plunger each day forces enough grease through the line to the bearing to assist in keeping the water at bay. All stuffing boxes will drip twice or so per minute and produce about a cup full of water per day; if they are over-tightened to stop this drip then the bearing and shaft will probably suffer from excessive wear.

PATENTED STERN BEARINGS

Patented stern bearings such as the unit marketed as the Deep Sea Seal have long been used on large ships but only in the past few years have they been installed in pleasure and work boats of all types. Our Australian office has, over the past 15 years, fitted hundreds and sold thousands of these units without any recorded failures. Halyard Marine in the UK formerly supplied the Deep Sea Seal model, however they now have the HMI seal which they claim is superior to the face type seal as used in the Deep Sea version. If you are intending to fit this type of device then you should investigate both types. See Suppliers Addresses in Appendix 3.

Your boat will require a bearing where the propeller shaft leaves the outer end of the tube. The tube generally protrudes through the hull by about 1–2 in (25–50 mm) and a bearing is needed in this end. The choice is between a fibre bearing, a tufnel bearing or a cutless rubber bearing. Cutless bearings are well proven and when properly set up with two small water scoops at the aft end of the tube (these scoops introduce water to lubricate the bearing), will give long and trouble free service. If the distance between the inboard stuffing box or seal and the outboard end of the tube is over, say, 6 ft 6 in (2 m) you may require an intermediate bearing generally known as a 'plummer block', in fact this may be a cutless bearing that has been forced half way down the tube. If your shaft protrudes from the tube by more than a few inches you may need a Y bracket bearing to support the outer end immediately ahead of the propeller. Decisions as to whether you need an intermediate bearing and similar questions are best addressed to the designer of your boat or other qualified marine engineer.

ROPE CUTTERS

These devices are designed to be clamped on your shaft just ahead of the propeller and can be very effective in cutting any rope or similar obstruc-

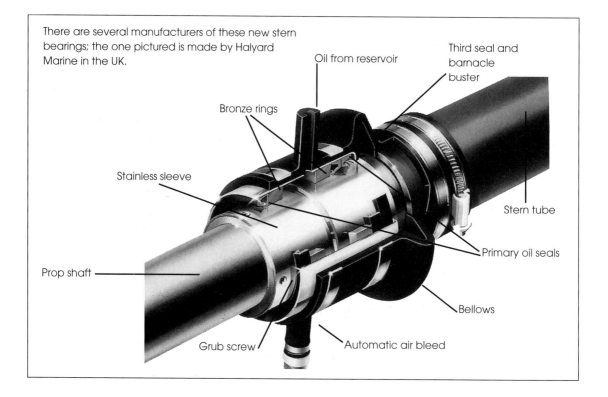

There are several manufacturers of these new stern bearings; the one pictured is made by Halyard Marine in the UK.

tion that would otherwise foul your propeller. There are several types available so get advice on the best one for your boat.

VENTILATION

Ventilation is another important factor for any engine and engine space. Your engine needs a considerable amount of fresh air so you need to install two vents of adequate size, one ducted below the engine to bring the fresh air in and the other ducted high up in the engine space to take the hot air out. Generally a blower is not required in the northern latitudes, however, in hot climates, you may need one to turn the air over at the correct rate. An engine space blower is simply a ducted fan that is designed to either import or export larger quantities of air than would circulate naturally. Vetus Den Ouden have a good range of these units and their catalogue will give advice on installation and use.

ENGINE COOLING

There are several different engine cooling methods including raw water cooling. This is usually found on older, slower-revving diesels; the method is to pump outside salt or fresh water through the engine casing and then out through the exhaust, cooling the engine in the process.

Most modern engines feature heat exchanger cooling; this method uses a special tank of fresh water which runs through the engine's cooling system; the fresh water tank contains internal piping and is in turn cooled by sea water being pumped through the pipes. This method protects the internal cooling system of the engine coming into contact with salt water; most modern diesel engines are cooled in this manner. One problem is that if the

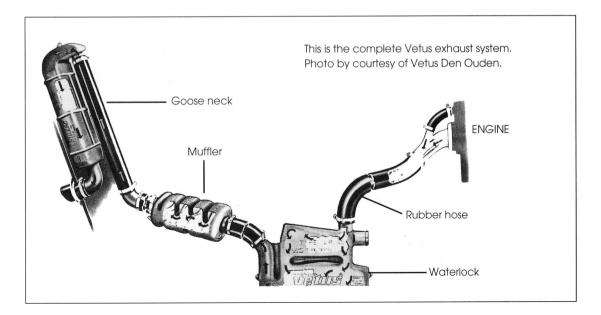

This is the complete Vetus exhaust system.
Photo by courtesy of Vetus Den Ouden.

Goose neck

Muffler

ENGINE

Rubber hose

Waterlock

outside intake for the cooling water becomes clogged then the whole system overheats; a sensor in the system can warn you before your engine seriously overheats.

There is a third method where no external water is required: keel cooling pipes are fitted to the outside of the hull, usually tucked in at the rabbet line. These allow the engine cooling water to recirculate and be cooled by the surrounding sea water. The most interesting version of this method is only possible with steel boats, or at least in boats that have a steel keel. It involves selecting a section of the keel and boxing this off to store the required quantity of a 50/50 mixture of antifreeze coolant and fresh water. This mixture is run through the engine's cooling system and, providing that the surface area of the selected portion of the keel is adequate to allow for the ambient outside water temperature, the system works extremely well. This latter arrangement employs two header tanks and works in a similar manner to the engine cooling system in your car.

An additional benefit of these engine cooling systems can be the incorporation of an insulated hot water tank, known in the UK as a calorifier. This tank has an internal pipe coil through which the hot water from the engine cooling system is run, and this in turn heats the domestic hot water. In *K*I*S*S* we found that running the engine for about 20 minutes every other day was sufficient to provide hot water for two days of showers, plus our other daily hot water requirements.

The internal cooling system where there is no outside cooling water, requires a lagged, dry exhaust. Considerable care is required in routing any exhaust line, especially the dry variety, which, despite the lagging, can get hot. If you have a dry exhaust then make sure that you pay particular attention to the ventilation of your engine space and the surrounding area. The principal drawback of this arrangement is that dry exhausts are usually noisier than the water-cooled systems.

Many exhaust systems involve the use of a water-lift muffler; salt water for engine cooling is fed into the exhaust tube just aft of where it leaves the engine and then into the muffler where the pressure of the exhaust gases forces the water out of the boat. This is among the quietest systems available; and quietness in your exhaust is a very desirable feature.

Choosing a system

If you are purchasing a ready-built new or used boat then the engine cooling and exhaust system will already be in place, and usually it is an expensive proposition to change from one system to another. If you are custom building then you should choose carefully; check other boats, weigh up the advantages and disadvantages of each system before you make your final decisions. Raw water cooling (no heat exchanger) is the least desirable because the innards of your engine are constantly exposed to the ravages of salt water or outside water containing all sorts of pollutants. Your choice should be between a system with a regular heat exchanger and where you use outside water to cool the heat exchanger and between a system where you have outside piping to allow keel cooling or a fully internal system. No matter which system you choose remember the advantages of having your hot water tank (calorifier) as part of the engine cooling system.

Water filters

If your engine uses water drawn from outside, either directly as raw water cooling, or by way of a heat exchanger, then you will require a water filter to remove any foreign matter that could damage the water pump impeller, or clog the cooling system and in turn cause the engine to overheat. The usual arrangement is to have the water filter located in line after the seacock where the outside water enters the system. The filter should be easily accessible as it should be checked daily and more often if you are motoring in weed or similarly infested waters. This unit is often made of clear plastic, presumably so you can see what is going on inside; do not let this discourage you from removing the top for regular inspections. Plastic sheeting which is one of the most common foreign bodies lurking in our waterways, is not always visible without removing the top of the filter. Most filters have a rubber sealing ring and you may find that a light coating of Vaseline will prevent the unit from sucking air. In any case, the rings will need replacement every two years or so. If you have a diesel-powered generating set then you should have a separate water filter for this unit; if possible locate the two filters so you can check both at the same time.

Water pumps

Your cooling system will include a water pump that is necessary to draw water from outside the hull and force it through the cooling system. The pump will include an impeller that will need replacing from time to time. Most water pumps are located in near inaccessible places; make sure you know where yours is located, and that you have a spare impeller and also check for difficulty of removing the impeller and covering plate. Speedseal is a product made in the UK and consists of a water pump cover that is attached with only one screw. This unit can be installed and removed with one hand so that it may be worthwhile to replace your regular water pump cover with one of these units.

SAIL DRIVES AND OUTBOARD MOTORS

Sail drives and outboard motors should not be considered for auxiliary power for any long-distance cruising boat. In the case of the sail drive, these are vulnerable if the seal between the leg and the hull fails; this in turn would allow an unstoppable amount of water to flood the boat. One manufacturer tried to overcome this potential problem by doubling up on

This Speedseal impeller cover would be a handy addition to any cruising boat.

the seal, similar to the double bagging one sees in the better class of supermarket! In the case of outboards, unless they are mounted in a well, even the long-shaft variety tend to cavitate due to the 'hobby horsing' habits of many small sailing boats when under power alone.

Outboards are mostly run on petrol or gasoline – not the best companion on a cruising boat. Apart from the danger of gasoline aboard any boat, we have all seen owners of small outboards trying to pull start these engines, they are notorious for not wanting to start at the most important time. Today there are many small lightweight diesel engines that can be fitted to all but the smallest cruising boat. If you have a very small cruising boat that you plan to use locally, then you may consider an outboard, but only if a small diesel inboard is beyond your means.

THE INSTRUMENT PANEL

Your engine will usually be supplied with an instrument panel and you may want to add to the standard instruments supplied. The minimum engine instrumentation should include a tachometer/revolution counter, engine hour meter, fuel gauge (notoriously inaccurate in boat installations – have a dipstick handy), volt/ampere meter. You will require an instrument light switch including a dimmer control for night use, an audible alarm as an indicator if you fail to switch off the ignition after the engine has been stopped, an engine stop button and a water temperature gauge. Some potential problems may be represented by warning lights and or buzzers; in my opinion, warning lights are not as effective as proper gauges. Audible alarms are recommended for water temperature, alternator output and the other 'vital life signs'. Your electrical panel complete with fuses is usually located in a separate box, however in some boats with inside steering it may be incorporated into the main panel.

FUEL TANKS

Diesel fuel tanks can be built from a variety of materials including stainless steel, glassfibre, aluminium or mild steel. Most builders choose regular mild steel. This material has the advantages of low cost, ease of fabrication and low maintenance requirements. The diesel fuel inside the tank takes

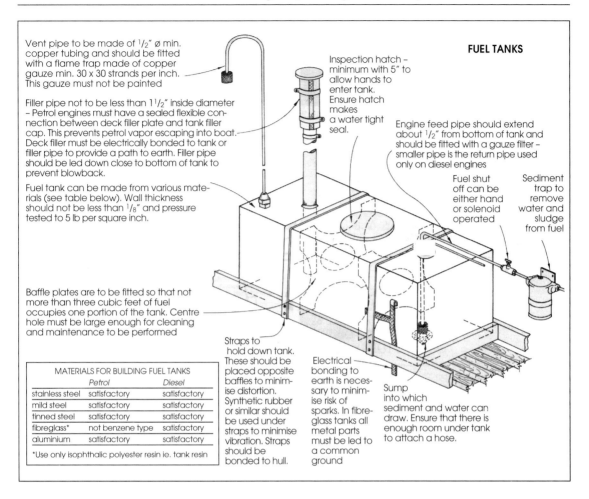

FUEL TANKS

Vent pipe to be made of $1/2''$ ø min. copper tubing and should be fitted with a flame trap made of copper gauze min. 30 x 30 strands per inch. This gauze must not be painted

Filler pipe not to be less than $11/2''$ inside diameter – Petrol engines must have a sealed flexible connection between deck filler plate and tank filler cap. This prevents petrol vapor escaping into boat. Deck filler must be electrically bonded to tank or filler pipe to provide a path to earth. Filler pipe should be led down close to bottom of tank to prevent blowback.

Fuel tank can be made from various materials (see table below). Wall thickness should not be less than $1/8''$ and pressure tested to 5 lb per square inch.

Baffle plates are to be fitted so that not more than three cubic feet of fuel occupies one portion of the tank. Centre hole must be large enough for cleaning and maintenance to be performed

Inspection hatch – minimum with 5" to allow hands to enter tank. Ensure hatch makes a water tight seal.

Engine feed pipe should extend about $1/2''$ from bottom of tank and should be fitted with a gauze filter – smaller pipe is the return pipe used only on diesel engines

Fuel shut off can be either hand or solenoid operated

Sediment trap to remove water and sludge from fuel

Straps to hold down tank. These should be placed opposite baffles to minimise distortion. Synthetic rubber or similar should be used under straps to minimise vibration. Straps should be bonded to hull.

Electrical bonding to earth is necessary to minimise risk of sparks. In fibreglass tanks all metal parts must be led to a common ground

Sump into which sediment and water can draw. Ensure that there is enough room under tank to attach a hose.

MATERIALS FOR BUILDING FUEL TANKS		
	Petrol	Diesel
stainless steel	satisfactory	satisfactory
mild steel	satisfactory	satisfactory
tinned steel	satisfactory	satisfactory
fibreglass*	not benzene type	satisfactory
aluminium	satisfactory	satisfactory
*Use only isophthalic polyester resin ie. tank resin		

care of the interior and providing you keep the outside well painted, your steel fuel tanks should give you long service.

If you are building or refitting an aluminium boat then you may find that the same material has been used for the tanks. There have been many problems with aluminium tanks. They tend to be susceptible to vibration and can fracture along the weld lines where baffles are attached inside the tanks. If you do use aluminium for tanks, make sure they are made from a high magnesium alloy such as 5083 or 5086 specification. Aluminium and steel tanks are sometimes built with the hull acting as one side of the tank. It is preferable to have the tanks built as separate units and tested before installation in the boat, so ensuring there are no leaks. Air pressure of about 3 lb per cu ft can be used to test the tanks; on no account simply hook up the tanks to a high pressure air hose or you may cause them to explode.

Capacity

Tank capacity is a subject on which there is often a difference of opinion between the designer, builder and owner. Most designers would like to

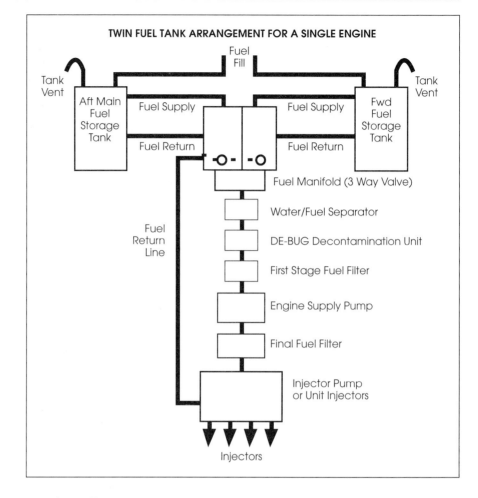

specify small, easy-to-remove tanks, the builder wants large tanks so that he can offer a cruising range greater than the competition, and the owner often requests an enormous cruising range under power.

If you have some choice, perhaps you are building or retro-fitting your boat, then choose tanks that give you a sensible cruising range. You will have already decided where you plan to cruise and how much motoring may be involved; if you live in an area where there are notoriously light or fickle winds then you will need not only a wardrobe of light-weather sails but also an adequate fuel capacity. If you plan to install a diesel-powered generating set, diesel cooking stove and/or a diesel-powered heating system, then take the fuel consumption of these items into your diesel fuel calculations. Remember that to avoid condensation and to minimise the chance of bugs infecting your fuel, you should keep your diesel tanks topped up whenever possible. As it does not make much sense to be carrying excessive weight around in the form of large amounts of diesel fuel, you should make careful calculations of your cruising requirements by estimating how much fuel you will need for engine running; add in the other usages as mentioned above before deciding on your fuel tank requirements.

Inspection

All tanks should be fitted with inspection hatches and be capable of being cleaned through these hatches. Fuel is drawn off by a pipe that enters the tank from the top and extends to within 25 mm (1 in) of the bottom. Arrange the tank and fuel line so that any sludge will collect below the drawing off line. A drain cock from the bottom of the tanks will allow you to flush out the tank. All tanks will need breather pipes, see drawing for these and other details. If you are purchasing a used or new production boat, your tanks may not meet all the criteria outlined in this chapter and may need attention in one or more areas, before you set out on a long distance cruise.

Flexible tanks

Another option you may want to consider is the installation of one or more of the collapsible tanks made from PVC or similar plastic material. These tanks can fit into awkward places; make sure the location for the tanks has a smooth lining and no projections that can cause punctures. Because flexible tanks may not last as long as those made of other materials, my opinion is that I would only choose this type of fuel container in situations where it was impossible or undesirable to install regular hard tanks.

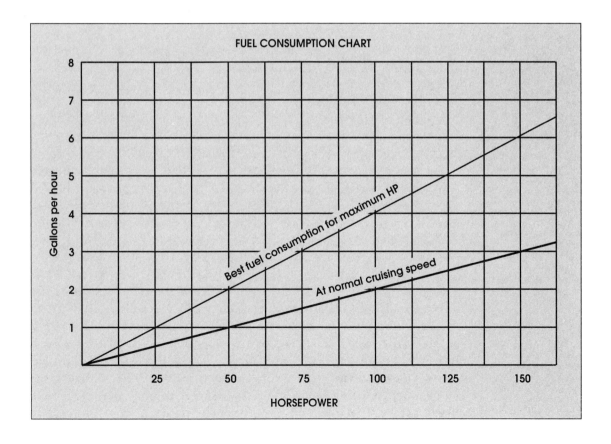

No matter what type of material you choose for the tanks that hold the fuel for your engine or any other liquids, make sure they are firmly anchored in place. The thought of a loose tank, either full or otherwise charging about the boat in a rough seaway should be enough to ensure you carefully check all tank supports and containment arrangements.

FUEL AND OIL FILTERS

Your engine will already be fitted with one or two fuel filters; these are installed by the manufacturer or company who converts the unit for marine use. These filters may be sealed and fully disposable or may be fitted with separate filters that you can replace at regular service intervals or as required; unfortunately most manufacturers now use the fully disposable type.

You should make sure your boat is fitted with an additional filter/water trap that will filter out most of the impurities including water *before* the fuel reaches your main filter(s). You will need to fit a fuel cock just before this filter so you can shut off the fuel when changing any of the filters. My preference was for the glass bowl type of water trap/fuel filter, however recently new regulations in some areas have insisted that an all-metal filter be installed. It is no longer easy to see if there is any water trapped in the system and required to be drawn off by way of the small outlet in the bottom of the filter; now one has to let out a small amount of fuel to make sure no water is present.

You will need to change oil and fuel filters at regular servicing intervals and in the case of a fuel blockage you may need to change fuel filters more often. As this is a very messy job, this is one area of boat servicing that you must understand and practise preventative maintenance wherever possible. When reassembling filter units, make sure you have the 'O' sealing rings in the correct order and position; sometimes the top and bottom rings look similar but are different enough to allow fuel or oil to leak out when the engine is fired up; start the engine with caution after servicing these items.

MICRO-ORGANISMS AND BIOCIDE ADDITIVES

All diesel fuel systems have the potential for micro-organism contamination and neglected or unprepared fuel systems will provide a breeding ground for these 'fuel bugs' once they are introduced into the system. These 'bugs' occur in the form of algae, bacteria, yeast, mould and fungi and this is a problem faced by all owners and operators of diesel engines no matter where the engines are located or in what type of transport the engines are installed. Boats used and laid up in warmer climates are more susceptible to the 'bug'; however, many cases have occurred in the UK and throughout USA and Australia. The problem is indicated by shortened fuel life, clogged fuel lines and increasingly corroded fuel system components and tanks.

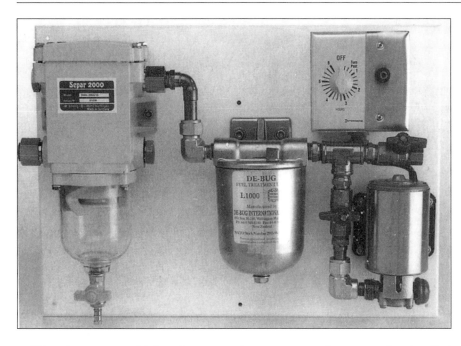

The De Bug™ 'fuel bug' filter comes in various sizes and has been used in all types of diesel powered applications both ashore and afloat. The smaller unit is capable of handling up to 35 gallons per hour (160 litres per hour). Larger sizes of this unit can handle amounts ranging from 265 gallons per hour (1205 litres per hour) through to 5000 gallons per hour (22,730 litres per hour), and remembering that a 97 per cent bug kill is claimed, then this is one of the most efficient pieces of equipment you could add to your cruising boat.

The degree to which micro-organisms grow and prosper in the fuel system is relative to how fast the fuel is used up and replenished. Boats with small fuel tanks or with high horsepower engines are less likely to have this problem than cruising sailboats with larger tanks.

If you leave your boat for extended periods, make sure that the fuel tanks are totally full. Partially empty tanks allow the bugs to thrive and water condensation to form; the *least* effect of this is that your water trap/fuel filter will be working overtime.

To avoid or eliminate bugs from your fuel it is necessary to understand how these pests thrive in your fuel tank. The various micro-organisms need water to survive, since they live at the interface between water and diesel fuel, using the fuel as a food source. Diesel contains carbon, hydrogen and dissolved oxygen, and is a good nutrient source for the bugs.

Once you have removed water from the system, preventative measures must still be taken against microbial growth. In a marine environment moisture is always present, and diesel bugs can grow quite rapidly. They can be present in the air, or in fuel taken aboard after you thought you had cured the problem. Some bacteria can grow into a mass many times their original size in just 24 hours. Other types can corrode fuel systems without being so obvious; these may show up as black grit resembling coffee grounds, either in the filter or in the water separator sight bowl (if you are lucky enough to have one).

If you purchase a boat that has been unused for some time then you would be wise to remove all of the existing fuel from the tanks and have them flushed out with fresh fuel before you use the boat. If in doubt about the cleanliness or if refilling after flushing out the tanks you should add a biocide chemical to your fuel to ensure any remaining bugs are destroyed before they multiply and clog your fuel system at some inappropriate moment.

There are many brands of biocides available and they have several factors in common. They are all expensive, usually costing around £20(US $32) for sufficient to treat a 150 gallon (680 litres) fuel tank. They are all composed of highly toxic chemicals, so highly concentrated that they need to be handled with utmost care. It is well to keep in mind that eventually, biocides lose their effectiveness and have to be replenished.

Micro-organism fuel filters

Those of us who plan to operate our boats in areas and under conditions where the fuel bug is likely to be an ongoing problem, may want to consider a more positive solution to micro-organism growth. Developed over 10 years ago in New Zealand, this new technology called De Bug™ Fuel Decontamination Unit uses patented and unique 'multi magnet' technology to kill micro-organisms. When correctly sized to the fuel flow of the particular engine installation this unit kills 97 per cent of the 'bugs' in a single pass.

The De Bug filter contains calculated magnetic fields produced by ceramic coated magnets located within the unit which destroy the micro-organisms as they flow through the filter. This unit is a one time installation, has no moving parts, no electrical power is required, no replacement filters and the only maintenance required is an occasional cleaning. Unlike the chemical biocides, the dead bacteria cells are destroyed in a way that does not result in a messy residue that can still clog filters. Do you need it? I do; after the experience of losing engine power in a rather embarrassing situation and all due to 'the bug', my boat is now fitted with this device.

CHAPTER 7

Marine Electrics

◆ *Glossary* ◆ *Electrical installations* ◆ *Solar panels* ◆ *Wind generators* ◆
Inverters ◆ *Generating sets* ◆ *Batteries* ◆ *Battery chargers* ◆ *Engine
starting battery* ◆ *Battery boxes* ◆ *Monitoring devices* ◆ *Cathodic protection* ◆ *Galvanic materials table*

B efore we start to discuss your boat's electrical system, on the following page is a glossary of terms that apply to this subject. Usually
these lists are located in appendices in the back of most books but I
feel they will be of more use to you in this chapter.

ELECTRICAL INSTALLATIONS

Unless you are well versed in the subject, this is one part of your cruising
boat where you should seek professional help. This applies to either fitting
or surveying your boat's electrical installations.

A boat is one of the worst environments for operating electrical appliances.
We are now adding more and more electrical items to our boats. It is advisable to make an early decision regarding just how many you have the capacity
for. A good guide is: the more extended your voyaging, the fewer electrical
items you will be able to successfully maintain under cruising conditions.
Look at it this way, operating electrical appliances takes power, the more long-
distance sailing you plan, the less motoring you may be doing, and the less
power generated by your alternator. The further you are from home the more
expensive are repairs and maintenance of electrical appliances.

Now having said that, I have to admit that many cruising sailors spend a
considerable amount of time either under power or motor sailing. Weather
conditions in certain areas of the world seem to dictate that more time is
spent motor sailing than in others. In the Mediterranean, many can be seen
under power or at least motor sailing. Chester and Norma Lemon told me
that they were obliged to motor sail or motor for about 50 per cent of the
time during their 50 000 mile cruise in their well equipped boat *Honeymead*.

If your cruising is local or coastal in nature, and your boat is large
enough, you will most likely want to consider having all the same goodies
on board that you use at home; I have nothing against modern electrical
appliances and labour saving devices; it is just that they may not mix well
with the practicalities of *long-distance* cruising.

GLOSSARY

AC (alternating current) 220 or 240 Volt (UK, Europe, Australia etc.) or 120 volt (North America) household power, shore power and also is the type of power usually supplied by your generating set. Some generating sets can supply 12 volt DC power, more on that later.

Ampere or amp or A The unit of measure of flow rate of current through a circuit.

Ampere-hour or Amp hour or AH A unit of measure of the battery's electrical storage capacity, obtained by multiplying the current in amperes by the time in hours of the discharge.

AWG American wire gauge.

AH Capacity The ability of a fully charged battery to deliver a specified amount of electricity at a given rate for a definite period of time. This number may give a false impression because you cannot use all of the AH or you will flatten the battery, and the AH capacity of any battery will vary with age and condition, see later in chapter.

Circuit An electric circuit is the path of an electric current; a closed circuit has a complete path and an open circuit has a broken or disconnected path.

Current The rate of flow that is best described by comparing it to a stream of water; the unit of measure is an ampere.

Cycle One discharge + one recharge = one battery cycle.

Dip switch A series of small switches used for alternate programming in all types of electrical and electronic devices.

Direct current or DC Power that is stored in any battery or supplied by an alternator or a 12V battery charger.

Discharge or discharging When a battery is delivering current, it is said to be discharging.

Equalise charge A controlled overcharge of the batteries which brings all cells up to the same voltage.

Gel cell battery A type of battery – it has the electrolyte in gel form.

Ground Used in automobiles when the negative battery cable is attached to the body or frame of the car, not recommended or generally used in boats.

ISO This is a European standard of wire sizes quoted in cross sectional area mm^2

LED Light emitting diode, often used as an indicator light.

Negative The negative terminal is the point from which electrons flow during discharge.

Ni-cad battery Nickel cadmium battery, rechargeable and used in small appliances, larger varieties are too expensive for most boats.

Ohm A unit for measuring electrical resistance.

Ohm's Law as you become more involved in studying your boat's electrical system you may wish to refer to these formulas.

Voltage:	$E = I \times R$	or $E = P / I$
Current:	$I = E / R$	or $I = P / E$
Resistance:	$R = E / I$	or $R = E^2 / P$
		or $R = P / I^2$
Power:	$P = E \times I$	or $P = I^2 \times R$
		or E^2 / R

E = VOLTAGE in volts. I = CURRENT in Amps. R = RESISTANCE in ohms. P = POWER in watts

Positive Opposite to negative.

Volt The unit of measure for electrical potential.

Here are two simple equations that you should write in your log and learn by heart.

• VOLTS multiplied by AMPS = WATTS
• WATTS divided by VOLTS = AMPS.

Watt The unit for measuring electrical power, a measure of the amount of power required by a particular appliance for example a 60 watt light bulb.

Wet cell battery The type of battery that uses liquid as an electrolyte, you add distilled water to this type of battery.

	TABLE OF POWER USAGE								
Appliance	Typical wattage	5 Min	15 Min	30 Min	1 Hour	2 Hours	3 Hours	8 Hours	24 Hours
13 in colour TV	50	0.5	1	2	5	9	14	37	110
VCR	50	0.5	1	2	5	9	14	37	110
19 in colour TV	100	1	2	5	9	18	28	74	221
Lamps / 100w	100	1	2	5	9	18	28	74	221
3 ft 'Fridge.	150	–	–	2	5	9	14	37	110
Blender	300	2	7	14	–	–	–	–	–
$3/_8$ in Drill	500	4	12	23	–	–	–	–	–
Microwave	900	7	21	41	83	–	–	–	–
Coffee maker	1000	8	23	46	92	–	–	–	–
Vacuum cleaner	1100	8	25	50	101	–	–	–	–
Toaster	800	6	20	–	–	–	–	–	–
Mid size fan	10	–	–	0.5	1	2	3	8	24
Stereo	50	–	1	2	5	9	14	37	–
Computer	100	1	2	5	9	18	28	74	--

The figures above represent what various appliances would use in amp hours during the periods shown. Check these numbers against the figures quoted for your appliances.

Before you work out how you are going to satisfy your waterborne electrical requirements, you must decide exactly what electrical appliances and devices you are going to install in your boat. The easiest and best way is to take the worst-case power draw, and make estimates from the literature or better still the nameplates of the appliances you are planning or have already installed. Make an estimate of how many of these items are running at any one time and take 100 per cent of this total; now select a power source, generating set, solar panels, wind generator or other alternative that will supply at least 80 per cent of the total load. As generating sets prefer to be run at least 40–75 per cent of their capacity; you may be forced to actually waste electricity if you overestimate your requirements!

SOLAR PANELS

These items are useful in keeping the battery charged when the boat is left unattended. Solar panels have been successfully installed to run all types of appliances including small refrigeration units. Solar panels (when they produce one amp or more) should always be run through a regulator so

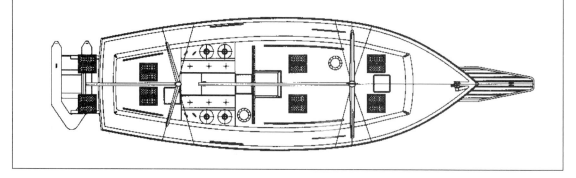

Locations for solar panels on boat. There are many areas of the boat where you can place solar panels; some locations are more suitable depending on your deck layout. If possible avoid high traffic areas.

that there is no chance of overcharging the battery. These devices are capable of *taking power out* of your battery; so make sure you prevent a reverse flow of current by installing a blocking diode for each panel or bank of panels; each diode uses 0.4 amp so remember that when calculating input. If in doubt, have the units installed by a competent person. You will need to understand the workings of all of these items so make sure you are around when the 'experts' are working on your electrical system. You can gain as much value from asking questions and absorbing knowledge as you can from having the work performed on your boat.

Solar panels are becoming more efficient and can be mounted on many areas of your boat. You will need to study the position of the sun in relation to the intended location of the panels. If you are able to rotate or angle the panels to take account of the boat's position in relation to the sun you will have a better chance of optimising the amounts of electricity generated by your panels. You would probably soon tire of adjusting the angle of the panels several times each day so you should calculate a reasonable angle to suit the area where you are sailing or moored and settle for around 75 per cent efficiency. When mounting the panels make sure you allow air to circulate around the whole unit, otherwise the excessive heat generated will seriously decrease the panel's output.

Once you have made the initial investment the power you receive is free. Most solar panels have a long maintenance-free life, usually 10 years or more. As with most other capital expenses you will need to decide if you will receive a reasonable return on your investment. In the case of solar panels, if you plan to cruise at least 25 per cent of the time then they are a good investment, if you are cruising only weekends and holidays then it would be best to only install a small unit that is capable of topping up your batteries when you are away from your boat.

Commercially available solar panels can produce power from 0.30 amps which are ideal for battery replenishment when you are away from the boat (one panel per bank of batteries); this set will avoid the need for a regulator in the system. Larger panels can produce up to 3.5 amps which can be arranged to form a charging system ideal for the offshore sailor. Most cruising folk who consider solar power as a serious source of electricity, install several panels designed to produce a total of around 20 amps. Select solar panels whose rated voltage, *at the temperature where you are operating*, is at least 14.8 volts (this allows for the blocking diode 0.4 amp voltage loss) to give net voltage of 14.4 volts which is the current required to fully charge lead acid batteries.

In many cruising boats it is possible to generate 30–40 per cent of your electrical power using solar power, add a wind generator and the figure can be nearer 80 per cent. These figures are for electrical requirements over and above that normally provided by the alternator when the engine is in use.

The sketch shown suggests locations for solar panels on your cruising boat. Each area has some advantages and disadvantages and you would only need to choose one or two of the suggested locations to provide the power suggested earlier. For instance, the panels on the fore cabin top that are located aft of the mast will be partially shaded by the mast and boom and may be prone to damage when a member of the crew is working around the mast. On boats with a pilot house the house top makes an ideal location. Boats with a long trunk cabin top aft of the mast provide an area out of the way of traffic, and in harbour the boom can be swung out of the way to allow the panels to receive full sun. An aft cabin top is a good location for panels. On aft cockpit boats the 'bimini' or other cockpit shading arrangement can be used to mount the panels. Finally davits, if you have them, are another possible location, they are out of the way and are not subject to shading.

Both cruising boats below are fitted with the minimum number of solar panels required to keep their batteries topped up. The glassfibre Halberg Rassey (outer) and the steel Roberts 44 *Sifu* owned by John Clark have made several Atlantic crossings. Note the pilot house and pram hood on respective boats.

To summarise, if you plan to have a serious solar panel installation then you must aim for the following:

- Reduce your daily electrical consumption to reasonable levels say 60 AH or less.
- Install sufficient panel area to generate 60 to 80 per cent of your requirements (this figure may include your wind generating capabilities).
- Make sure you select panels that have sufficient output, taking into account operating temperatures and power loss.

- Keep the surfaces of the panels clean and free from salt spray.
- Do not depend on having to regularly change the angle of the panels (this will soon become an unbearable chore), mount the panels where they will obtain maximum sun for the maximum amount of time.

WIND GENERATORS

Many cruising sailors argue that wind generators are more efficient and are more cost effective than solar panels. I see no reason why you cannot install both types of generating equipment and then you will reap all the benefits offered by both systems. Other than initial cost there are virtually no disadvantages of having solar panels or a wind generator aboard your boat so why not have both systems? The subject of initial cost should be considered in the same light as mentioned previously, if you use your boat for more than 25 per cent of the year, these charging devices are a sound investment.

The thought of those blades whizzing around will ensure that most people consider the safety aspects installing a wind generator. To prevent damage to the charging unit and/or to the blades, some units need to be shut down when winds reach over 30 to 50 knots. Other manufacturers include automatic speed control and shutdown; you should look for these features as stopping the blades in high winds could be a risky operation. Most generators that you will be considering will have blades of around

Wind generators like this Aerogen 4 manufactured by LVM can be mounted on a pole or off the mizzen mast.

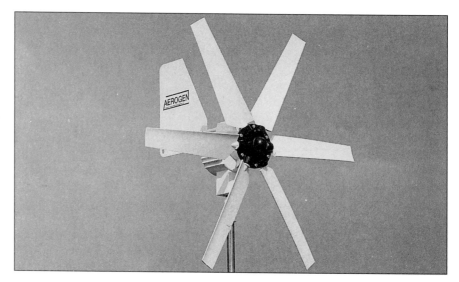

5 ft (1.5 m) diameter. Do not let these comments put you off considering a wind generator, they are a wonderful source of electricity on any cruising boat but they must be treated with respect.

Wind generators do make noise; how much noise depends on the model and I have noticed over the years that they are becoming increasingly quieter as each new model appears on the market. The number of blades does not usually increase the output but it does make for a quieter unit. Try and inspect the various models under operating conditions and see for yourself how much, and what type of noise is involved.

Wind generators will require some maintenance, they are basically electric motors running in reverse so they have all of the same components as an electric motor. Brushes and even bearings will need periodic replacement; check with the manufacturer on what maintenance procedures are needed and how often replacement parts are required for their particular unit.

Calculating the power generated

You can calculate the amount of electrical power you will receive from any wind generator. Many years ago, it was calculated that the maximum efficiency that could be extracted from the wind would be around 59 per cent. With any mechanical device there are losses due to friction of the moving parts and it has been estimated that the average efficiency from wind generators is 30 per cent or better; some manufacturers claim higher efficiency ratings of up to 50 per cent. Although cruising boats need the wind to operate, it is a fact that we tend to try and avoid the places where the wind blows hardest. If you study the wind speeds of the areas where you intend to cruise, then you will invariably end up with a number of between 10 and 15 knots *average* wind speed. The formula is as follows:

Watts = 0.0653 × 30(%) × blade diameter in metres squared × wind speed in knots cubed.

For example: (12 amps) 152 watts = 0.0653 × 0.30 x 1.52 × 1.52 (1.52m blade squared) × 15 knots^3

The same calculation based on a wind speed of 10 knots would give a result of 45 watts or 3.75 amps.

It is obvious that wind speed is one of the most important factors when calculating output – more important than the diameter of the blades. Make sure you estimate the correct average wind speed when evaluating the performance of these wind machines. It is worth remembering that a wind generator can be operational 24 hours a day and may be producing electricity long after the sun has gone down.

INVERTERS

It is well to note that inverters are users rather than manufacturers of electricity; they simply take one form of power and turn it into another; they keep a little for their trouble; the best models only consume around 5 per cent to undertake the conversion process. There are several manufacturers of these appliances, see Appendix 3.

It is becoming more common to have a combination battery charger/inverter in one unit. Inverters perform in the same manner, either as a stand-alone unit or as part of a combination charger/inverter appliance.

There are many inverters available that are capable of converting the 12 or 24 volt power stored in your battery bank into 220/240 or 120 volts AC and they are generally available in sizes ranging from 50 watts to 2500 watts. If you are intending to run most of your electrical appliances from 120 V or 220 V/240 V AC power supplied by your inverter, then before you purchase you will need to know the total power requirements of the appliances that you plan to run at any one time. If you have a relatively small boat and you are only intending to run one small AC appliance on AC power then a simple strip-based, 200 watt inverter may suit you best. One of these small units may cost you as little as £100 (US $150). For owners of larger, live-aboard cruising boats *it is a common mistake to underestimate requirements* so it is most important that you calculate your expected needs carefully and then allow some room for expanded usage. You will need the 12 V DC battery storage capacity to back up this usage so this will temper your appetite for AC appliances. Remember to convert your requirements to the same units, either amps or watts, before you start to estimate your total usage, see the conversion formula at the start of this chapter.

With certain limitations an inverter that converts 12 V to 120 or 220 V AC can make life easier for those who want to run AC electrical appliances aboard their boats. In early models the current produced by inverters was not the same as that supplied to your home by the local power authority.

Combination inverter / battery charger units like this Freedom model made by Heart (USA) take up a suprisingly small amount of room for the power and convenience they provide aboard any cruising boat.

The inverter produces a square, stepped or what is generally referred to as a modified sine wave. An on-board generating set and your local power company delivers pure sine wave power. Why do you need to know this? Because the inverter-manufactured 120 V or 220 volt power may not run certain appliances properly; problems will occur when inverters are coupled with TV screens, computer screens, radar screens and similar units. Even as I write, these problems are being addressed and largely overcome, however it is wise to check with the inverter manufacturer regarding the compatibility of their unit with the appliance you wish to operate. In the past two years there has been a vast improvement in the way inverters operate so you should be able to find one that will suit your requirements and that will give you trouble-free service.

When considering which appliances you can run on your inverter, you will need to consider the 'starting' amperage required by many pieces of electrical equipment. An electric drill that operated successfully on 1000 watts will normally take a considerably larger amount of power during the first few seconds of operation; this is sufficient time to create an overload situation and trip out the whole circuit. Because inverter technology is constantly changing, you will need to investigate the various makes and models to ensure that the unit you select will perform the functions you require.

GENERATING SETS

For those who plan long offshore passages and require considerable electrical capacity to power their various pieces of equipment, a suitable sized generating plant is worth considering. You should first consider if your needs can be met by a combination of solar and/or wind generated power combined with the output of the alternator attached to your main engine. If you still require more electrical capacity, then a diesel-powered generating set will be your next option. There are three types of power generating sets capable of making the large quantities of AC electricity demanded by a collection of modern appliances. You may select a fully installed diesel powered unit, or a unit that is driven by a power take-off from the main engine, or a portable petrol/gasoline powered unit. There is one additional type of gen set and this unit is unique in that it generates large quantities of 12 V DC power as opposed to most units that deliver 120 V or 220 V AC power. Although you may use some AC power aboard your boat, most of the electricity generated by a 120 V or 220 V AC unit is converted to 12 V DC (via battery charger) before it is used on your boat; perhaps it may be better to start off with a 12 V generating set and only convert the minimum amounts to 120 V or 220 V AC via an alternator. This 12 V gen set is discussed later under its own heading.

The portable units are inexpensive but are not suitable for the serious cruising vessel; they are very noisy, introduce petrol/gasoline aboard and are not up to powering the typical range of appliances on board.

For those on a budget, a PTO (power take-off) generator could be the answer. PTO units have a centrifugal clutch arrangement enabling them to keep generating at varying engine speeds. Units, including the M90 Marine Cruising Generator which is made in the USA, are capable of producing considerable output; units of 3–6.5 Kw (3.75–8 Kva) are readily available. This produces enough power to keep most appliance-minded cruising families happy. Those that plan a large amount of motor sailing will find this a satisfactory solution to their electrical generating needs.

If you have considered using your main engine and the regular alternator as a primary source of generating 12 V DC power, it is as well to remember that you should have some load on the engine; in other words it is not recommended to run your diesel engine at low revolutions without some load being applied. Some cruising people, when needing to recharge batteries whilst tied to the dock and where shore power is unavailable, run the engine at low speed but with the transmission engaged and thus letting bollards, cleats, warps and jetty take the strain; this practice is not recommended if you want to return to that marina in the future.

For the larger boats, a conventional diesel powered generating set, usually referred to as a gen set, offers power at a reasonable price. These units can supply AC power starting at around 3 KVa up to any size that you could require. Make sure you choose a unit that is powered by a water-cooled diesel engine with at least two cylinders. The entire unit must be either already installed in a well-insulated cabinet or capable of being insulated and contained in a soundproof box. Most units are reliable and deliver the amount of rated power promised by the manufacturer; the difference between a 'good' and 'best' is the amount of sound emitted. Try and hear one example running before you make a final decision. With a well-insulated unit, the main sound problems can come from the exhaust water rather than from the diesel or the generating unit; it is possible to overcome this by using a 'water lift' type exhaust system so the water exits

(LEFT) Large capacity alternators like this Balmar Power Charger can add 75 to 200 amps to your charging system (RIGHT) Apollo 12 volt Diesel Generator, 130 amp output. This unit was custumbuilt to include a high pressure pump for a reverse osmosis water maker system and a refrigeration compressor for an engine-driven cold plate system for ice box refrigeration.

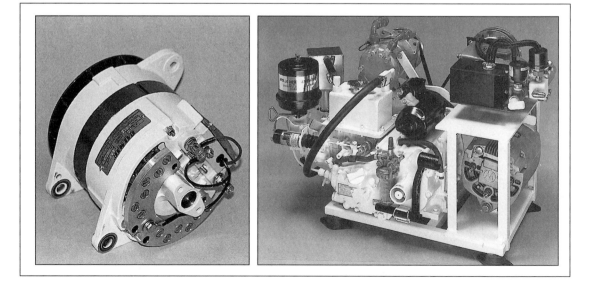

the hull below the waterline. Compared to the main engine, these units are quiet, fuel efficient and can be tucked away in otherwise unused space in the engine compartment. No matter how quiet and efficient your gen set, you will not want to run it more than, say, two hours each day. Vetus Den Ouden and many other manufacturers in Europe, USA and most other parts of the world offer a range of these units at affordable prices.

All 12 V DC generating system

Now we come to the fourth option mentioned earlier; the generation of large quantities of 12 V DC power. This solution does make sense when you consider that most appliances likely to be found on even the most completely (electrically) equipped cruising boat can be run on 12 V DC power. As part of considering this option you would need to be prepared to install a larger amount of battery storage than you would need when using other charging arrangements.

At time of writing I am unaware of any assembled 12 V DC generating sets being available 'off the shelf', however as all of the major components are readily available you should not encounter any insurmountable problems custom-building a unit to suit your particular requirements. If you are planning to use an all (mostly) 12 V DC system then you will need a battery capacity in the top end of the estimates I have quoted later in this chapter. If you opt for this system you can plan on installing twice the amp hour battery capacity of your daily usage and needless to say, you will need to include a monitoring device which includes an amp hour usage meter.

Most cruising boats that have a regular AC generating system fitted need to run it two to three hours per day. With the all 12 V DC system it is estimated that you should only need to run your generating set for the same amount once every two to three days; this alone should be sufficient to encourage you to consider this system. One disadvantage is that it requires much heavier wiring and fuses. The main requirement of this system is that you must be able to charge larger than usual amounts of 12 V DC power so that your batteries can be replenished at the rapid rate necessary to balance the two or three day usage in the two or three day charging cycle. Your 12 V charging system will need to be able to produce between 150 to 300 amps *per hour* to make the system work: it can be done.

The charging end of the unit will consist of one or more high output alternators coupled with a dedicated, suitably-sized, water-cooled diesel engine. The recommended procedure is to decide how much output you will require to charge your batteries in the desired time; match the output of the alternator to this requirement and then select a suitably-sized diesel engine. Between 10 and 20 hp should be sufficient to power the alternator(s). The engine will not require a transmission unit but you will need to have a shaft that can be bolted to the flywheel and this in turn will accept the one or two pulleys used to drive the alternators via a suitable V belt arrangement.

A reliable regulator will be part of this system – the last thing you would want to do is to cook those extensive and expensive batteries. You will need to have the entire unit housed in a sound-proof box similar to that used for an AC gen set. The cost of this 12 V DC generating set should not exceed the cost of a similarly sized AC (120 V or 220 V) unit so your decision can be based purely on the convenience factor and on the requirements of your electrical system. For details of the availability of high output alternators, see equipment suppliers in Appendix 3.

BATTERIES

Lead acid batteries

Lead acid, *wet cell* batteries are mainly used on cruising boats and not the ni-cad variety which are generally too expensive to be considered by most of the cruising fraternity. Later in this section I will outline some of the claims made for *gel cell* batteries; you can choose either type with the knowledge that 50 per cent of the battery 'experts' will agree with your choice.

In Europe, batteries are sized by quoting amp hours and in the USA the size may be quoted as a 'D' followed by a number; for example D8 refers to a 220 AH battery. As the 'D' sizes are not always consistent between manufacturers you should enquire further to establish the actual storage capacity of the particular battery.

% of capacity	At rest	No rest
100	12.8	12.7
90	12.7	12.6
80	12.6	12.5
70	12.5	12.4
60	12.4	12.3
50	12.3	12.2

This table shows typical battery voltage at different states of charge/discharge.

Traditionally the batteries have been divided into two or more banks, one for engine starting and one or more banks to serve your domestic requirements which includes everything *except* starting the engine. If you are planning long-distance offshore voyaging rather than local coastal cruising, your electrical requirements, and especially the methods of satisfying those needs will be different. When coastal cruising, you will often have access to shore power so you can not only conserve your battery power but also top up your batteries using your battery charger.

For domestic use you will most likely have more than one battery; when this is the case your installation is referred to as a battery bank. When arranging a bank of batteries, it is preferable that all of the separate batteries are of similar or better still of the same amp hour capacity; one reason for this is that if the sizes vary then the smallest battery may control the system, it may halt the charging process when it is fully charged and before its larger companions have even neared that state.

The following estimates of suggested battery capacity are not to be taken as recommendation of actual amp hour requirements but rather to give you an indication of the numbers involved. If you are planning to carry the appliances that many of the cruising fraternity consider as necessities you can use these numbers as a starting point. Based on boat length and assuming there is a crew of two to four people, you are most likely to require the following domestic battery amp hour storage capacity:

28 ft (8.5 m) 150 – 250 AH   35 ft (10.6 m) 400 – 600 AH
45 ft (13.7 m) 800 – 1000 AH   55 ft (16.7 m) 1200 – 1500 AH
65 ft (19.8 m) 1500 – 2000 AH.

The connections between separate batteries are made in *series* or *parallel*; these terms refer to the way in which two or more batteries are connected one to the other. If you require large battery capacity, there is a sensible limit to the size of each individual battery. Unfortunately when considering large capacities it is seldom possible to keep each individual unit to a size easily handled by one person, however do give this some consideration when arranging or re-arranging your batteries. If you have more than one 12 V battery and you want to create a bank of batteries, then you would connect these batteries in parallel so they remain and act as a 12 V battery unit. If you want to create a 24 V battery (often used on larger pleasure and many commercial boats) then you can connect two 12 V batteries in *series*, or 12 V when you connect two 6 V in *series*. Golf cart or similar 'deep cycle' heavy duty batteries are often available in 6 V and are becoming more widely used to make up large battery banks where large amp hour capacities (for example 2000 AH) are required. By connecting batteries in *series*, you can create up to 48 V DC, which is usually seen only on large commercial boats. Most cruising boats will have a number of 12 V batteries connected in *parallel* to form their domestic 12 V battery bank.

The batteries you choose for domestic storage should be the 'deep cycle' type; these batteries are constructed differently to those used for engine starting. Deep cycle batteries are designed and built to accept a moderate load over an extended period; the plates are thicker, the cases are usually heavier and they are better equipped to accept regular discharges, up 50 per cent, and then be recharged on a regular basis. You will need to decide the number and sizes of domestic (house) batteries you wish to carry. If you make a careful estimate of your daily use in amp hours and multiply this amount by four then you will be on the right track. Remember that you must balance your battery capacity against your power usage. It takes considerably longer to put back the amperage you take out of the battery than it does to use it. Batteries do not accept recharge at the same speed as they will accept discharge.

A 12 V battery in operational condition will read more than 12 volts. If using a voltage meter, you take a reading soon after you have discontinued the charging process and your meter will most likely register 13 plus volts. After a few hours (without any discharge due to usage) your battery will read 12.8 volts if fully charged and somewhat less if it has not reached full capacity. A battery that reads 12.2 volts is 50 per cent discharged. A battery that reads 11.6 volts is almost fully discharged and may be damaged beyond further use.

Ni-cad batteries

Ni-cad batteries have been used as domestic batteries on boats and they were already installed on *K*I*S*S* when I purchased her. These batteries worked well on this relatively 'low tech' (electrically speaking) boat, however, they are extremely expensive to replace. It is unlikely that any boat you purchase will be fitted with this type of battery. Ni-cads are reputed to have an extremely long life so it may be worth investigating them if you are building a new boat or totally refitting an existing one.

Gel cell batteries

Gel cell batteries are lead acid batteries and are similar to the common wet cell battery but differences in the chemistry and construction provide some unique features. There is no need to add water and the tops of these batteries stay clean. Unlike wet cell batteries, the gel will hold its charge for months if left sitting with no load and no float charge. They can be stored in the off-season without the constant float charge and without fear of freezing. The gel cell battery will accept a higher rate of charge and usually delivers better performance when connected to an inverter than the wet cell variety. The combination of acids in the gel cell prevents sulphation and eliminates the need for battery equalisation.

Finally do not confuse *gel cell* batteries with the so called *maintenance free batteries*. These hold the liquid electrolyte in a sponge like material and water cannot be added; they are totally unsuitable for marine use.

Gel cell batteries are considerably more expensive than the regular lead/acid type and some 'authorities' do not favour them. I have mentioned them here, so you can research the matter further. They may be worth the extra money to you, this will depend on how you feel about their longevity.

Equalizing batteries

This method of rejuvenating your batteries is one that should only be considered if you feel comfortable with your system and when you consider you have the experience to handle the process with complete safety. While a battery is being discharged sulphuric acid in the electrolyte reacts with the lead plates in a chemical reaction which produces electricity and lead sulphate. When the battery is re-charged, electricity flows back into the battery and causes the reverse chemical reaction which turns the lead sulphate back into lead and sulphuric acid.

With each discharge and recharge cycle, a small amount of lead sulphate will remain on the plates. If this sulphate is left in place for very long, it will harden and or crystallize and eventually reduce the battery's capacity, increase the internal resistance and destroy the battery's ability to deliver an adequate amount of power. When this occurs, even an equalize charge cannot remove the sulphate and the battery becomes useless except for re-cycling purposes. However there is a way to counteract the build-up of excess lead sulphate – if you want to learn more about this process and receive exact instructions as to how it is carried out, see Appendix 1 and you can also contact Heart Interface, see address in Appendix 3.

BATTERY CHARGERS

There are a great variety of 12 V DC battery chargers capable of delivering between 5 and over 100 amps to your electrical system. Most battery chargers are operated on 120, 220 V or 240 V AC (mains-shore power or are generated via your AC generating set) and are often left running when you are connected to either source. It is a fact that when you try and run a 240 V AC battery charger on 220 V (for instance when you take your boat abroad to mainland Europe), you will find that it most likely will only deliver 80 per cent or less of its rated output. You should choose a battery charger with an output matched to your expected requirements from that source. The amount of amperage you need from your charger will be calculated at the same time as you are allowing for amperage income from other sources such as engine alternator, solar panels, wind generator, etc.

Battery chargers do not deliver their full output until the battery is absolutely fully charged; for example, if you are charging a battery via a 30 amp battery charger and assuming your batteries are 50 per discharged at the start of the cycle, you will note, via your charging gauge, that the needle immediately registers 30 amps input. After a period (depending on the capacity of the battery bank), the input amperage needle will drop back to 20, 15, and eventually to 1 or 2 amp input. This is how most battery chargers are designed to work; they will give your battery as much power as they are designed to deliver until the battery reaches say 80 per cent of capacity and then the input is much slower. You will note that if you turn on a 12 V DC appliance during this period when the charger is not delivering full capacity, then the charge will increase to cover the amount of amperage you are using. I have found this feature useful when estimating the amperage used by a particular appliance.

Your battery charger is usually fitted with a sensing device that controls the rate of charge delivered from the charger to the batteries. The sensor is connected via a cable first to your domestic batteries, because they use the most power. A second sensor line is connected to the engine starting battery so that it will also be kept fully charged. The sensor is needed to ensure that the batteries do not become overcharged; if the readings are taken in the wrong order (engine battery first) then the charger will stop delivering power as soon as that battery is fully charged, in this case the domestic batteries would be left only partially charged. Once the sensor detects that the batteries are fully charged, and assuming that the charger is still activated, then it delivers a 'float charge' to keep the batteries topped up as required

The internal setting in your battery charger will determine how many volts your charger can deliver; this is usually preset by the manufacturer but it may be possible to alter the setting. Please check with the manufacturer before you start making changes to these settings; if your charger delivers too high a voltage it can cause your batteries to 'boil' or 'gas' and you may permanently damage them. When grossly overcharged, batteries have been known to explode so take precautions when working on your batteries; as a minimum safety measure, always wear protective clothing and eye glasses.

ENGINE STARTING BATTERY

In the past it has always been a rule that the engine starting battery should be capable of being totally isolated. One reason is that you may want to leave the *domestic* battery system switched on to power an automatic bilge pump, alarm or similar device. In some cases you can wire bilge pumping and alarm systems directly to the battery so they are not accidentally turned off when you leave the boat.

The construction of the engine starting battery is different from that of the deep-cycle type used for domestic purposes. The plates are thinner and they are designed to deliver short bursts of high amperage to crank your engine. Once the engine is running, the charging from the alternator quickly replenishes the amperage that was used when you started the engine.

This is one reason why, when you check your engine start battery, you will often find that it is fully charged. In fact, you must be careful not to overcharge this unit; your regulator is designed to prevent this happening. Because this battery seldom gives trouble (it always cranks the engine and generally performs as you would expect), it is sometimes neglected. Make sure you regularly check the level of the water (electrolyte), the voltage level and general condition of the battery.

As batteries have become more reliable there are some experienced cruising folk and battery 'experts' who argue that it no longer is necessary to divide the battery banks into domestic and starting units. If you have a generating set with its own starting battery this can be worked into an arrangement where, in the event of your engine-starting battery becoming flat, you can fire up the generating set (using its own starting battery) and using the main battery charger, put sufficient charge into the engine battery to get the engine started and the system recharged. In a worst-case scenario, you could always use the generating set battery to start the main engine via a set of jump leads.

BATTERY BOXES

Hopefully, the first time you are in rough weather is *not* the time you decide that your batteries need to be installed in a better manner. Batteries complete with fluid weigh around 0.875 lb (0.4 kg) per amp hour capacity; a 220 amp hour (called an 8D in USA) battery weighs about 160 lb (76 kg) so it does not take much imagination to envisage what would happen if one of those monsters breaks loose in a seaway. Batteries need to be installed securely and the best way is to house them in their own box. A battery box can be built out of ¾ in (20 mm) waterproof plywood and is best lined with fibreglass so that any spills are contained. The box should be bolted to, or otherwise securely fastened to, a suitable structural member.

When selecting the location for your batteries, remember that they may (and probably will) need to be removed or exchanged for new ones, during the time you own the boat. If the batteries are not fitted with strong straps, make sure you install straps under them so you can remove the batteries from the box. Although many authorities insist on a *vented* lid I believe that provided the batteries are strapped in place, they are unlikely to jump out of the box and the open top is better for ventilation; more importantly it is one less obstacle to regular checking of the battery fluid levels and keeping the terminals and top of the case absolutely clean. If you are considering a large battery storage capacity, then you should try to locate at least a large percentage of your batteries in the keel or bilge area; if you do so, you will need to make sure they are isolated from any possible contact with bilge water.

FIXED BATTERY MONITORING AND MEASURING DEVICES

For those (like myself) who need to know the exact state of their batteries and associated equipment at all times, there are, at last, a number of monitoring instruments that can be permanently installed in the electrical system and provide instant information on demand.

The E-Meter is manufactured in the USA by Cruising Equipment (see Appendix 3) and is marketed in the UK under the name of The Heart Link 10. The E-Meter is an instrument which measures most of the battery functions that will interest you; for instance it measures ampere hours, voltage, current flow, the time remaining until the battery would be discharged. The amount of energy remaining in the battery can be displayed as an amp hour number on the LED display, or as a percentage of the battery capacity. The meter measures the system voltage and the current is measured via a 500 amp, 50 millivolt shunt supplied with the unit. The 'time remaining' function tells the user how long the battery will last at the present rate of discharge. The meter is powered by the battery system to which it is attached; the drain is so low as to be disregarded in most systems.

This meter has been extensively tested by several boating magazines and various interested bodies and the results and comments have all been extremely favourable. The unit comes with extensive documentation so you should have no problems setting it up to work on your boat. Your

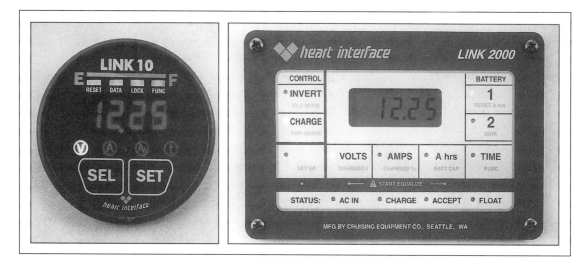

(LEFT) The Heart Link 10 is one of the best value battery monitoring devices. (RIGHT) If you have a large bank of batteries or more than one the Link 2000 may suit you best.

electrical system will be well served by this device with the constant monitoring of your batteries voltage, amps, amp hours remaining and general state of health. All of this for only £188 or US $199.

The E-Meter supports a number of additional features which may not be of interest to the average cruising sailor, including the ability to connect to a RS232 port which allows it to communicate with a computer thus enabling data to be recorded as required. Another feature is the ability to be connected to a data logging device by the same manufacturer; this unit can in turn be connected to a GPS.

There are many other battery monitoring devices available that will enable you to be advised on every battery function; I have mentioned the E-Meter/Heart Link 10 because it represents such outstanding value for money. There are battery monitors that have even more functions than the E-Meter and you may find these useful.

Volt meters

A hand held volt meter is a must; most of these instruments not only read volts on the DC and AC scale but also ohms and amps. Most units are capable of reading a wide range of voltages from a small percentage of one volt through to 500 volts AC or more. On a cruising boat, the main interest will lie in the 12 V DC, the 120 V AC or 220 V AC ranges. Volt meters are available in two basic configurations, analogue or digital. Like many people I started off with an analogue instrument. However I soon found that the digital version was capable of reading or perhaps more correctly, being read to a more accurate degree. These instruments are relatively inexpensive and good quality instruments are available for as little as £15 (US $22), so you can probably afford to own both types. Either of these instruments can be used to test circuits and are the first instrument you would reach for (after you check the fuses!) when any electrical appliance or instrument fails to operate.

Hydrometers

Another measuring instrument that you should have on board is a hydrometer; this device consists of a glass tube with a rubber bulb on one end and a thin tube on the other. Inside is a glass float marked off in one or more scales. It is used to draw off a small amount of fluid from each cell to give a reading to determine the amount of charge present in a particular cell. If one cell registers a considerably lower reading than another, you may well have a problem not only with that cell but with the battery as a whole. One dead cell will render the whole battery useless causing it to need replacing.

Many hydrometers also have a scale to measure specific gravity; this scale can be used to test, among other things, the state of the coolant in your engine heat exchanger system. As temperature can play a part in the operation of your batteries, some hydrometers are fitted with a thermometer; in my opinion this is over-kill and there are less expensive ways of determining and factoring in the temperature.

The fluid you draw off the battery when testing with a hydrometer will contain a high sulphuric acid content; this liquid is capable of burning your skin and eyes so *make sure you are adequately protected*. Your clothing and fabrics used in the interior of your boat are especially vulnerable to even the smallest amount of battery acid so be careful when using your hydrometer to test battery cells. Always rinse out the instrument in fresh, clean water after use; do not put contaminated water down the sink; use a separate glass jar for rinsing and dispose of the water in an appropriate manner.

Thermometers

Excessive heat is a great way to destroy your batteries and a battery should never be charged when its temperature is in excess of 45° C or 120° F. In a hot engine compartment, there will be higher temperatures than outside so you will need to be aware of this before attempting to 'fast charge' your batteries. It is possible to fit a small thermometer on to each battery, this is in turn linked to a warning device to let you know if your batteries are threatened by overheating. If one or more of your batteries feel hot to the touch then you should investigate further.

CATHODIC PROTECTION

Protection against galvanic corrosion is needed when different metals are close to each other; seawater acts as an electrolyte forming a galvanic cell and electrical current flows from the least 'noble' metal to any higher up the scale (see Galvanic metals table) causing corrosion in the less noble metal. To avoid corrosion of props etc you can fit a *sacrificial anode* made of zinc or magnesium to your skeg which will corrode more readily than fittings made of metals higher up the galvanic scale. Cathodic protection is

ABYC STANDARD E-2, GALVANIC SERIES OF METALS IN SEA WATER
(Sea water flowing at 8 to 13 ft/sec. (4.8 to 7.8 kn.),
temperature range 50°F to 80°F (10°C – 26.7°C) – except as noted)

Metals and Alloys (Anodic or Least Noble–Active)	Corrosion-Potential Range in Volts
Magnesium and Magnesium Alloys	-1.60 to -1.63
Zinc	-0.98 to -1.03
Galvanized Steel or Galvanized Wrought Iron	NA
Aluminium Alloys	-0.76 to -1.00
Cadmium	-0.70 to -0.73
Mild Steel	-0.60 to -0.71
Wrought Iron	-0.60 to -0.71
Cast Iron	-0.60 to -0.71
13% Chromium Stainless Steel, Type 410 (active in still water)	-0.46 to -0.58
18-8 Stainless Steel, Type 304 (active in still water)	-0.46 to -0.58
Ni-Resist	-0.46 to -0.58
18-8, 3% Mo Stainless Steel, Type 316 (active in still water)	-0.43 to -0.54
78% Ni – 14.5% Cr – 6% Fe (Inconel) (active in still water)	-0.35 to -0.46
Aluminium Bronze (92% Cu – 8% Al)	-0.31 to -0.42
Naval Brass (60% Cu – 39% Zn)	-0.30 to -0.40
Yellow Brass (65% Cu – 35% Zn)	-0.30 to -0.40
Red Brass (85% Cu – 15% Zn)	-0.30 to -0.40
Muntz Metal (60% Cu – 40% Zn)	-0.30 to -0.40
Tin	-0.31 to -0.33
Copper	-0.30 to -0.57
50-50 Lead – Tin Solder	-0.28 to -0.37
Admiralty Brass (71% Cu – 28% Zn – 1% Sn)	-0.28 to -0.36
Aluminium Brass (76% Cu – 22% Zn – 2% Al)	-0.28 to -0.36
Manganese Bronze (58.5% Cu – 39% Zn – 1% Sn – 1% Fe – 0.3 MN)	-0.27 to -0.34
Silicon Bronze (96% Cu Max – 0.8% Fe – 1.5% Zn – 2% Si – 0.75% MN – 1.6% Sn)	-0.26 to -0.29
Bronze-Composition G (88% Cu – 2% Zn – 10% Sn)	-0.24 to -0.31
Bronze-Composition M (88% Cu – 3% Zn – 6.5% Zn – 1.5% Pb)	-0.24 to -0.31
13% Chromium Stainless Steel, Type 401 (passive)	-0.26 to -0.35
90% Cu – 10% Ni	-0.21 to -0.28
75% Cu – 20% Ni – 5% Zn	-0.19 to -0.25
Lead	-0.19 to -0.25
70% Cu – 30% Ni	-0.18 to -0.23
78% Ni – 13.5% Cr – 6% Fe (Inconel) (passive)	-0.14 to -0.17
Nickel 200	-0.10 to -0.20
18-8 Stainless Steel, Type 304 (passive)	-0.05 to -0.10
70% Ni – 30% Cu Monel 400, K-500	-0.04 to -0.14
18-8, 3% Mo Stainless Steel, Type 316 (passive)	-0.00 to -0.10
Titanium	-0.05 to +0.06
Hastelloy C	-0.03 to +0.08
Platinum	+0.19 to +0.25
Graphite	+0.20 to +0.30

(Cathodic or Most Noble–Passive)

a subject that you will need to explore no matter where you cruise. Many people are under the false impression that boats that cruise exclusively in freshwater do not require any special form of cathodic protection. A C Duff, the UK experts on this subject, have produced two excellent pamphlets. One for boats operating mostly in salt water and the other for fresh water. These publications explain the special requirements needed to protect your stern gear, rudder and associated underwater equipment from the ravages of stray electrical currents and other mysterious gremlins that can damage your propeller, prop shaft, rudder gear and in some cases the hull itself.

These problems are not new; in 1681 Samuel Pepys noted in one of his diaries that the removal of lead sheathing on ships of the line, reduced the corrosion on the iron rudder posts. Over 100 years ago, experiments were conducted in this field and proved that when two metals were electrically connected and immersed in water, the resulting corrosion of one of the metals is speeded up, while the other receives some level of protection.

Gold, silver and platinum are the only metals found in the ground in their natural and indestructible form. All other metals are manufactured from ores by various processes and as such, they are prone to return to their natural state, unless protected in some way. It takes considerable energy to convert an ore to a metal but it takes *virtually no energy* to allow the metal to return to its natural state; we have all seen unprotected metals such as steel or aluminium react in this way.

If you study the table showing the most noble metals, gold, through to the least noble, magnesium, you can better understand how the presence of two dissimilar metals in certain environments can set up a process that will literally reduce one of the metals, while offering at least some form of protection to the other.

If you wish to study marine electrics further the subject is fully covered in several specialised books, see Appendix 2.

CHAPTER 8

The Tender

◆ *Inflatable friend or rigid companion?* ◆ *Stowage*

Those of you who have previously cruised from marina to marina and now plan to voyage further afield, may be surprised to learn that experienced cruising people consider the choice of a tender one of their most important decisions. In many of the most desirable cruising areas, marinas are few and far between. An unsuitable dinghy can limit the places you visit, or in the worst case it can put you or your vessel at risk.

There are two main types of dinghy, inflatable or rigid. Within these two main types are several sub species and you will find a wide selection of all types on display at any sizeable boat show.

INFLATABLE TENDERS

Inflatables offer a great selection of sizes and types; when you think of a dinghy this may be the first type that springs to mind. Do not take this as an automatic endorsement of the inflatable, you should consider all the options. The recently developed semi-rigid inflatable (RIB) which has a fibreglass bottom and inflatable sides could be of interest to owners of larger cruising boats. This type is widely used by rescue services and has all the attributes of a deep V planing hull plus the advantages offered by the inflatable chambers that make up the sides. Most of these RIBs are too large to be used as a cruising boat tender; however if your boat is over, say 55 ft (16.7 m) you may wish to consider this option.

In recent years there has been a large increase in the number of inflatable manufacturers. Until a few years ago it was a simple matter of choosing between an Avon, Zodiac or more recently a Tinker. These brands still dominate the market but there are other choices that may save you money while still providing you with a serviceable dinghy. New ranges of the different brands are constantly being changed and upgraded, you will need to explore these before making a final choice.

Once you have decided to use an inflatable, you will need to decide what capacity is required. Providing it does not strain stowage arrangements, you should choose the largest size to meet your needs. Most cruising sailboats should carry a dinghy that will comfortably carry the expected number of crew and a reasonable number of stores in one or two trips from the shore to the boat. The load-carrying capacity is governed by two main factors, diameter of the buoyancy tubes and length overall. Inflatables with tubes that are less than 1 ft (305 mm) in diameter should be rejected, the best dinghies have a tube diameter of around 1 ft 3 in (381 mm). You should stay away from the single chamber inflatable, a single puncture could spell disaster; this rules out the cheapest versions of most manufacturers' ranges.

Check for the following desirable features:

• Well designed rowlocks
• Sturdy oars
• Rope hand holds on the sides
• A reinforced towing eye.

The floor can be a single layer of the hull material, fully inflatable or plywood panels. Most experienced cruising people prefer the inflatable or slatted versions; the large ply panels offered with some models are hard to fit and a nuisance to stow. The importance of some form of floor will become apparent the first time you try and stand up in the dinghy, an action that is often required when transferring crew and stores to and from the dinghy.

The material is of utmost importance; it will govern how long it will last and how well it stands up to rough usage. The buoyancy tubes are made from a layer of synthetic cloth to which a water-resistant coating is applied. You should check if the coating is applied to both the inside as well as the outside. The basic material is usually nylon or polyester; nylon is the heavier material but polyester is more likely to retain its shape.

The coating is either elastomer Hypalon, neoprene or a plastomer like PVC. The PVC is the cheaper coating and you will find it on many of the inexpensive inflatables. One problem with PVC is that it is not as UV resistant or resistant to chafe as a elastomer-type coating and for this reason the manufacturer's guarantee is usually shorter for the PVC coated models. The construction techniques required to make an inflatable using the elastomer coating are more labour intensive, so adding to the cost. If you intend to cruise in sunnier climes or in the tropics then the elastomer-coated version with its superior UV resistance may be worth the extra money. For cruising in northern areas the less expensive PVC-coated version may be your choice.

It is important that an inflatable is easy to row and comes with substantial oars. For my own use I prefer the traditional timber type which are supplied with some Avon models. You may want to fit a small outboard. Your choice of mountings will be between an inflatable with a plywood transom or one where a pipe frame is used to support the outboard bracket. Which type you choose may depend on dinghy size and the expected number of times you expect to use the outboard. Many yachtsmen prefer the plywood transomed versions because the tubes tend to extend past the transom and give the dinghy better directional stability and balance. Most inflatables will accept outboard power in the order of 2–5 hp and these engines should be capable of reaching speeds up to 8 knots when matched to the correct size of inflatable and carrying a moderate load.

Some dinghies are fitted with an inflatable keel, this helps with directional stability under both oar and outboard power. Don't forget to check the valve arrangements; can they get lost? Are they easily replaceable? How does the pump work and how long does the dinghy take to inflate using the supplied equipment? All of these will be a measure of the dinghy's quality.

There are other considerations: for instance, do you intend to sail it (Tinker, Metzler)? Use it as a primary or secondary life raft (Tinker)? If you intend to sail your inflatable, make sure you are given a demonstration on the rigging arrangements. A Metzler I once owned was satisfactory to sail but was so complicated to rig, that we only sailed it on one occasion.

At several boat jumbles I have seen multi-patched inflatables sell for inflated prices (excuse the pun) and if you are planning an extensive cruise, this is one item that you should buy new. It is possible to find a used dinghy that still has a considerable life expectancy but often you will find that the going price seems to be near to what you would pay for a similar new one when purchased through one of the discount outlets.

RIGID TENDERS

Rigid tenders come in a wide variety of types, sizes and materials. No matter which material you select, make sure that the dinghy has built in buoyancy so that in the event of swamping, it will still be capable of supporting the crew until it can be bailed out. The choice of material lies between glassfibre, sheet plywood, moulded veneer or aluminium. I have seen very presentable steel dinghies in Holland; these could be considered for boats over 55 ft (16.7 m). The glassfibre versions will generally have a round bilge and conventional shape although pram style dinghies are produced in every shape imaginable. Plywood dinghies are generally of the pram type and many owe their heritage to the Sabot and similar designs that are used to teach sailing to children; these are excellent sailers but may not row as well as other types. Over the years I have seen many beautiful round-bilge clinker-planked, timber, or plywood tenders, however, as I am no lover of maintaining a lot of varnish work, I have resisted the temptation to own one of these beauties.

Even if you envisage using an outboard as a primary power source, the dinghy should be easy to row. Small outboards are notoriously unreliable so the ability to be rowed by any member of the crew is one of the first criteria for a dinghy. The flat-bottomed, pram type dinghy is easy to stow, sails well but is difficult to row in anything of a chop. The V-bottom version handles a little better under oars but not so well as a conventional dinghy.

In Australia aluminium dinghies, or 'tinnies' as they are known, are very popular. These tenders come in a variety of shapes and are usually formed in large presses and riveted or welded to make a very light, serviceable tender. If you can acquire one of these unique dinghies you will be converted. They are capable of taking the type of beating that goes with being

hauled up rocky beaches and accept other abuse that is part and parcel of acting as a tender to a serious cruising boat.

The best type of solid dinghy is conventionally shaped with a shallow V or, better still, a round bottom and a small skeg that runs from just aft of the forward end of the waterline to the transom. This type will row, sail and perform well under power. You may want to consider a 'nesting' dinghy, that is a two piece tender where one end fits into the other. This type takes up less room and may be easier for you to stow in the space available.

No matter what material your solid dinghy is made of, or what design, you will have to consider its weight. It most certainly will be a problem if the dinghy cannot be launched and retrieved by one person. Another consideration is some form of gunnel protection so that the dinghy and its mother ship (and other yachts) are all protected from each other. There is no time to be fiddling with fenders when coming alongside in anything of a seaway.

The rigid 8 ft (2.4 m) dinghy pictured is ideal as a tender and can be built in glassfibre or plywood by any competent amateur. Note the two sets of rowlocks; ideal for alternative rowing positions, depending on the load being carried.

DINGHY STOWAGE

As you go about selecting your dinghy you will need to decide where and how you intend to stow it. In the case of an inflatable it may be acceptable to have it deflated during long passages but you should make provision for stowing it partially or fully inflated at other times. Strong sunlight is the enemy of all inflatables so to ensure the longest life expectancy make sure you keep it covered when not in use. In most areas towing a dinghy is a nuisance to yourself, and in some cases, to others so do not count on this as an option. Many cruising boats carry the dinghy inverted on the deck or cabin top; if you can find room to stow your dinghy like this then this is a reasonable

Note the rigid dinghy securely stowed in davits on this Roberts 36. This boat was built in Yugoslavia before the recent troubles; I wonder where it is now.

Dinghies should be stowed upside-down when sailing offshore or in bad weather. Davits that automatically stow the dinghy in the inverted position are available.

alternative. Larger boats can carry the dinghy the right way up in chocks; however except in the largest craft, this arrangement would seem imprudent.

Using a folding dinghy as the only ship's tender is usually restricted to smaller craft or to those where stowage is at an absolute premium. The folding variety may be suitable where only infrequent use is required and this type makes an excellent second tender. If fitted with a sailing rig, this dinghy can be used as a source of amusement and training for the younger members of your crew.

Davits are another alternative and many long-distance cruising boats have used this method to stow their dinghy. But, a large breaking following sea could fill the dinghy so this stowage option may not be a good idea except for coastal cruising. Some larger boats now have dinghy garages in the stern, if your boat is over say 55 ft (16.7 m) then this arrangement may be worth exploring, especially, at the design stage.

The opinion of most experienced cruising people is as follows; for gunkholing, local, coastal or inland water cruising, the inflatable tender is adequate. For the long-distance voyager who needs a dinghy capable of carrying large loads of people, water, fuel and stores as well as absorbing rough treatment, a rigid tender is preferred. If you have room to stow an inflatable as well as a rigid dinghy you will be equipped to handle all eventualities, including the day you have to row out a heavy kedge anchor and chain. If you plan a small outboard for powering your dinghy, one solution may be to store the petrol tank in a self-draining locker similar to that used for the butane or propane gas bottles.

CHAPTER 9

Ground Tackle and Warps

◆ *Types of anchors* ◆ *Selecting chain and line* ◆ *Other hardware*
◆ *Anchor weight* ◆ *Anchor winches* ◆ *Chain stowage and anchor
lockers* ◆ *Cleats and bitts* ◆ *Mooring lines* ◆ *Fenders* ◆ *Buoying the
anchor* ◆ *Where to anchor*

If you are presently cruising locally, then your boat will most likely be covered by a comprehensive insurance policy. Unfortunately you are in for a severe shock when you start to enquire about purchasing cover for your boat which includes a long-distance cruise. Armed with the knowledge that very few cruising boats are lost at sea and those that come to grief are mostly lost when at anchor; you should pay serious attention to the entire subject of anchoring and associated gear. Even if you can afford to fully insure your boat (and yourself and crew) you will still appreciate the feeling of security afforded by adequate anchor(s), chain and line all collectively known as *the ground tackle*. Do not underestimate the seriousness of this subject; it is all too easy to be complacent when sitting in a marina or lying in a snug anchorage.

Apart from the times where you are forced to anchor off a lee shore or in an open harbour, in a howling gale, there will be other times when you are ashore and you cannot even get back to your boat. If your vessel cannot be left on its own in all but the most threatening and inclement weather, then you will never feel free to accept many invitations ashore and you will miss out on many of the most enjoyable aspects of cruising. So let us consider what equipment you will need to be able to anchor your boat safely in the conditions you are likely to encounter once you venture offshore. As experienced cruising adventurer Alan Lucas put it 'When you drop anchor you must be able to say "I have arrived" and not "I am here as long as the anchor holds."'

ANCHOR CABLES

The serious offshore cruiser may carry the following inventory:

- Main anchor 300 ft (90 m) short-link tested chain, matched to your

ANCHOR TYPES

You will need two bower anchors (one main and one spare). Both can be of the plough type or you may choose one plough and one 'Bruce'. If your boat is over 40 ft (12.2 m) then a heavy fisherman type may be advisable. You will also need a dinghy anchor and a grapnel for retrieving fouled chain and line.

ADMIRALTY PATTERN OR FISHERMAN'S ANCHOR

This is the style of anchor that comes to mind to non-boating people when the word anchor is used. It has fallen out of favour with the cruising fraternity but it does have some desirable features.

This anchor will hold in almost any bottom but it does have some drawbacks. The fact that one fluke projects above the ground makes it subject to fouling when the vessel swings, due to a change in wind or tide. As a stern anchor, the admiralty pattern has a lot of merit and under these conditions the head of the vessel will be secured by your main anchor. In conditions where lack of space or other factors make it desirable to moor the vessel fore and aft, then you may find the Admiralty pattern anchor very much to your liking. As this anchor needs to be collapsed for convenient stowing, it will have to be 'made up' before it can be reset.

CQR OR PLOUGH TYPE

These were, until recently, the most commonly seen devices gracing the bows of many

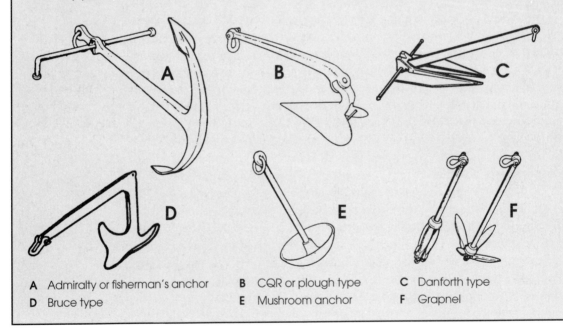

A   Admiralty or fisherman's anchor   B   CQR or plough type   C   Danforth type
D   Bruce type   E   Mushroom anchor   F   Grapnel

winch gypsy and marked at regular intervals so you can judge the amount you have laid.

- Two 50 ft (15 m) lengths of the same chain to act as leaders for the anchors fitted with rope line or cable.
- Three 300 ft (90 m) heavy nylon lines for use with second bow or stern anchors. You may want to consider having these lines on spools to facilitate handling and stowage.

For the coastal cruiser or one that is too small to reasonably carry the cruising boats. Several new and redesigned types have in part usurped the CQR as the most popular cruising anchor. If you have limited knowledge in this field then you could choose this pattern for your main anchor, knowing that it has been a well proven friend to thousands of cruising sailors in the past.

This anchor is easy to stow either on a specially short bowsprit/anchor roller or on deck. It even stows readily into a reasonably sized anchor or chain locker. If you could only carry one anchor then the CQR or plough type would be the one to choose. (Make no mistake, *never* carry only one anchor; even the smallest cruising boat will need a back up anchor and accompanying chain and or line.) Faults in this type of anchor are rare, but, very occasionally a weakness will show up in the form of a crack in the casting where the shank meets the bow; make sure you inspect this area regularly. To summarise the attributes of the CQR, it holds well in mud and sand, needs care when setting it in weed, and it should be seriously considered when selecting your number one anchor.

DANFORTH AND DANFORTH TYPES

Danforth type anchors are a good choice for your number two anchoring system; they hold well in mud or sand. They have only one main weakness and that is in the size and strength of the shank. I have seen several which sported very distorted shanks while the rest of the anchor remained intact. There are some which are made entirely of high tensile or stainless steel.

This anchor stows flat but does have a number of corners to catch lines at awkward moments. If you stow it on deck, make sure it is secured in proper chocks and is out of the way where it is unlikely to catch sheets. Most cruising people agree that they would choose a Danforth as their second anchor.

BRUCE ANCHOR

This is a more recent development and has gained a lot of admirers at the expense of both the CQR and the Danforth patterns. The Bruce has similar characteristics to the CQR but it is a one piece unit and has some benefits. The Bruce sits well on any well designed bow roller arrangement and should be considered for either your number one or two anchor.

MUSHROOM ANCHOR

This is used on those occasions when you intend to stay for a long period and where no satisfactory permanent moorings are otherwise available. The anchor would be most likely made up on location and not carried on board. You may not trust the local moorings and as it is usually impossible to inspect them thoroughly, even by diving, you may decide to create your own. If you do decide to lay your own mooring then make sure you have adequate *very* heavy chain laid out from the mushroom anchor especially if you intend to turn this mooring into an all-weather haven. You must use a suitably sized swivel between the end of the heavy chain and your regular mooring chain.

CORAL ANCHOR

An anchor called a 'coral pick' was used for for anchoring into reefs. With the increase of cruising and diving boats, this caused considerable damage to coral outcrops and is now discouraged.

inventory suggested above you can modify this list to suit your requirements.

Chain is not necessarily the strongest anchor cable available but it is the most widely used and for many good reasons. Chain is resistant to chafe where it lies over rocks and whatever else is lurking on the bottom ready to cut, chafe or otherwise separate your boat from your well set anchor. If you are intending to cruise far from home then it is recommended you carry at least one set of all chain ground tackle. Make sure you select adequate size chain (see suggested sizes below), inspect it regularly and replace it when it shows any sign of wear. All shackles should be secured using soft stainless wire. As with anchors do not stint on the cost of this item.

Rope can be used in combination with chain to make up your second set of ground tackle. As mentioned earlier, two sets of all chain make for the best security, however if weight is a problem or if you carry a third anchor, then a rope/chain combination is acceptable. The chain should be about 25 per cent of the length of the total. Again pay particular attention to shackles, splices and other joining arrangements.

Recently, woven-nylon, reel-mounted lines have come on the market; the idea is to mount one of these units in the cockpit or near the stern. These and other similar arrangements can be acceptable only in addition to your two main fore and aft sets of ground tackle.

The bitter end

Unless you are a student of nautical terms, or an experienced sailor, you have probably heard this term and wondered what it meant. The bitter end is the inboard end of the anchor chain which should be attached to a eye in the anchor locker or to another appropriate location. The safest way to attach the bitter end to the strong point is to lash it on with several turns of strong line; the lashing should be of sufficient strength to take the strain in the event that you accidentally let all of the chain run out of the locker. The reason for lashing and not bolting or using a shackle is that in an emergency you can 'slip' the chain by cutting the lashing.

When choosing anchor chain, you may use the following sizes as a preliminary guide.

Boats LOA to 25 ft (7.62 m)   ¼ in (6 mm)
Boats 25 ft to 30 ft (9.14 m)   / in (8 mm)
Boats 30 ft to 40 ft (12.19 m)   in (10 mm)
Boats 40 ft to 50 ft (15.24 m)   ½ in (12 mm)
Boats 50 ft to 60 ft (18.29 m)   in (15 mm)

The exact chain sizes will depend on your intended cruising grounds and the conditions you are likely to encounter.

ANCHOR WEIGHT

For your main anchor (non-specialised types) you can budget for a unit that weighs 1 lb for each foot of your boat's overall length (1.5 kg per metre of boat length). If you are planning extensive stays in foreign parts where you may have to rely exclusively on your ground tackle, then you should carry at least one anchor that is double this guideline. More accurate weight guide- lines can be recommended by the manufacturers of the various types of anchors. Excellent performance figures have been compiled in recent years from the extensive testing undertaken for and by the various boating magazines.

ANCHOR WINCHES

Once you are equipped with the correct number and types of anchor you will need to turn your attention to the methods used to lower and more importantly raise the entire set of ground tackle. In my early days of sailing, the boats I owned were not equipped with anchor winches; these were considered devices required by old men! Now that I am an *older* and, hopefully, a wiser man, I pay a lot of attention to selecting the correct anchor winch and associated equipment. My current attitudes make anchor handling, if not a pleasure, at least not too onerous a chore.

Hand-operated anchor winches come in a wide variety of types and sizes and it is impossible to list the most suitable type for every type of ground tackle. If you select a well known brand that has been proven over a number of years, and seek the manufacturer's advice, you will be well on the way to making the right choice. The two-speed variety offer obvious advantages.

If your boat is over 40 ft (12.2 m) or if your crew is not physically strong or your pocket is deep enough, then either an electric or hydraulic anchor winch is worth the investment. In any case make sure that the winch can be operated both mechanically as well as in its powered mode.

When setting up your anchor winch make sure the chain and gypsy are perfectly matched otherwise you will be forever clearing jams, and your gypsy will be subjected to undue wear. Vetus Den Ouden and other winch manufacturers offer matching winch/chain combinations and these are worth your consideration.

Anchor handling should be as easy as possible. The leads between the winch and the anchor roller must be arranged so that there is the minimum of friction caused by any unfair leading of the chain. The bow rollers should be as large as practical and arranged so the chain cannot

This formidable anchor windlass was made by Herbert Fritz and is set up to handle the twin anchors fitted to his 53 ft (16 m) steel sailing boat *Kallisto*.

jump out when you are winding it in, or as it runs out. If you do not have an anchor bowsprit then make sure the anchor rollers project as far forward as possible, this will avoid damage to your topsides.

OTHER ANCHORING HARDWARE

Here are a few items to assist in safely anchoring your boat:

- An electric anchor light, with a hurricane lamp as a back-up
- A good spot light for picking out hazards in the dark
- A pair of polarised sun glasses; you will need these to see the bottom in strong sunlight and they are great for picking out coral heads and other underwater obstructions
- Tested galvanised shackles for each anchor plus spares
- One coil of soft sizing wire
- One large shackle for running the weight of trip line down the main chain cable.
- Two heavy duty swivels, two heavy duty hooks – one shackled to ½ in (12 mm) rubber snubber
- A suitable buoy for marking the location of your anchor
- A bucket and brushes for scrubbing down the chain and anchor as it comes aboard
- Anti-chafe gear: a selection of anti-chafe gear will get plenty of use and should include, split heavy plastic pipe that will fit over chains, spare rags and cord to secure anti-chafe material in place.

There are many other items that are associated with anchoring such as depth sounder and a dinghy for laying kedge anchors, however these items are covered in some detail elsewhere.

CHAIN STOWAGE

Chain should be stowed as low as possible. As a designer, I am aware of the problems of getting the chain low enough but not allowing the chain locker to intrude too far into the accommodation. Perhaps it would be a good idea if the US Coastguard rule that there must be a watertight bulkhead 5 per cent aft of the forward end of the DWL, was a requirement for all cruising boats; this would provide an adequate chain locker. I favour an arrangement where the chain locker is divided by a fore and aft bulkhead, this could be an extra strength factor while allowing you to stow two complete sets of ground tackle without them becoming entangled as has happened to most of us on more than one occasion.

A deck-mounted chain pipe is a good arrangement since it funnels the chain down to where you want it and allows the opening to be closed off making an almost watertight arrangement. On *K*I*S*S* there are twin chain pipes each with a screw-down plastic cover that ensures absolute watertightness.

If the distance from the deck opening to where the chain enters its stowage area is an appreciable distance, then a sloped pipe will be required to guide the chain to its stowage destination. The pipe should be set at an angle and for quietness of operation, a strong plastic pipe is recommended.

ANCHOR LOCKER

The anchor locker is usually below decks so it has to be considered along with the accommodation layout. You will want to decide if you want the self-draining variety, that is one where the drains are at the bottom of the locker and where the locker is sealed off from the rest of the boat. Water can drain out but it can also flush in through the drain holes. I prefer a locker that drains via a pipe down to the area where the bilge pump is located.

Many cruising boats carry two anchors in the forward anchor locker but few are divided so that the rope anchor line and/or chains do not become mixed between the two anchors. Generally the main anchor, plough or 'Bruce' style is kept stowed on bow rollers or small bowsprit and ready for use. The secondary anchor, usually a Danforth type, is stowed in the locker along with its rope and/or chain. Some anchor lockers are arranged so that the chain runs through a tube down towards the centre of the boat thus putting the weight where it can contribute to the stability of the vessel. If you decide to arrange your anchor chain in this manner, make sure that you can gain access to assist the chain to stow neatly and also ensure that it cannot get loose in the event of a knockdown. In the case of a third anchor, you may want to consider carrying this at or near the stern where it can be useful in situations where you wish to anchor fore and aft.

ANCHOR CLEATS

It is most important to have an adequate anchor cleat, sampson post or other arrangement for securing the anchor chain. Simply letting the winch take the strain is not good enough. Make sure you have a method of securing the chain so it will not accidentally run out when put under extreme stress, or if something goes amiss with your winch. In the event that your vessel needs to be towed, you will need to have a very strong cleat or other arrangement for securing the tow line.

MOORING BITTS

On my own boat I prefer mooring bitts to cleats. Cleats are fine for sail handling and control but when you have the weight of the entire boat plus a surging action wanting to separate the line from your boat, then a well built set of bitts is preferred. Six of these fittings should suffice on boats up to 55 ft (16.7 m), one pair up near the bow, one pair amidships and another near the stern. These bitts make the best termination for your mooring lines and will provide a perfect arrangement should you decide to

Note the substantial mooring bitts positioned to give a fair lead to mooring lines.

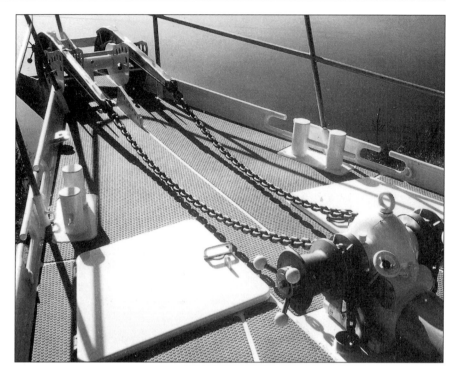

take your boat through some of the canals and waterways of Europe, the USA and elsewhere.

MOORING LINES

You will need a variety of mooring lines and warps. At least two of these lines should be two and a half times the length of your boat, add another four lines that are one and a half times your boat's length and finally two that are about the same as your boat's LOD. There are several types of synthetic line available and each has its advantages and drawbacks. I prefer plaited lines similar to the ones used for sheets.

FENDERS

If you are to protect your boat from external damage when you are in harbour or especially when travelling through any of the world's waterways, then you will need a good supply of fenders. The most sensible type are home-made from small car tyres that are covered with a fabric to keep the black off your topsides. If you prefer the bought variety then choose a dark colour. In any case you will need at least five per side and if you are very protective towards your topsides you could consider a 'horse blanket' type of cover that is slung between your topsides and the fenders. Fender socks look great on boats that are seldom used but they soon become tatty with constant use.

Boarding plank

A boarding plank can be used as the ultimate fender. When lying alongside a wall where there are intermittent posts, normal fenders will not do the job. The plank – a builder's scaffold plank works well – is fitted with a hole each end so it can take a line and be slung outside the fenders to keep your topsides free from damage.

BUOYING THE ANCHOR

If you feel there may be debris, or other anchor chains present, it is recommended that you buoy the anchor. Use a trip line so you can come up on to and over the anchor and then trip it using the buoyed line. This may also have another use if you have to slip your anchor in an emergency; you may be able to return and recover your anchor at a later date. It is a good idea to mark your buoy 'Anchor buoy only – do not touch', hopefully this will stop someone else from using your buoyed anchor arrangement as a mooring when you are asleep, or temporarily away from your vessel.

CHOOSING AN ANCHORAGE

Deciding where to anchor is one of the most important decisions you will have to make each time you reach a new port. You may be tired, relieved to have reached this destination and tempted to drop the hook at the first likely spot. Not a good idea, you must seek out a safe spot that has reasonable access to the shore. You will most likely find that the best spots are already occupied by the locals!

When selecting a location to anchor you should look at the availability of facilities such as dinghy landing as well as negative factors such as the proximity of shipping movements and obvious dangers such as wrecks and reefs. You should consider the direction of likely adverse weather, and exposure to wave action, length of fetch, the depth of water and the tidal range. You will need swinging room to avoid the shallows, other craft, fairways and wrecks.

Before you set your anchor in the spot that you hope will be your location until you are ready to move, you must ascertain the type of bottom. Your choice may lie between mud, sand, or less desirable heavy weed, general debris or old moorings. Hopefully your pilot book will provide answers to some of these questions.

CHAPTER 10

Safety

◆ *Lightning protection* ◆ *Fire extinguishers* ◆ *Alarms and detectors*
◆ *Flooding* ◆ *Bilge pumps* ◆ *Float bags* ◆ *Abandoning ship*
◆ *Lifejackets and life vests* ◆ *Liferafts* ◆ *Safety lines* ◆ *Man
overboard* ◆ *Radar reflectors* ◆ *Emergency steering* ◆ *EPIRB* ◆
Firearms ◆ *Smuggling* ◆ *Dress code*

It recently occurred to me that safety should be spelt as *preparation*. Many, but not all accidents can be avoided by careful preparation and those that cannot be avoided can be mitigated by previous planning.

As the owner and/or skipper of your cruising vessel you are responsible for the safety and well-being of yourself and your crew. Assuming that you are familiar with all of the safety devices and equipment aboard your boat, the next step is to make sure you pass on this knowledge to every person who is aboard your boat *before* it leaves the dock. It would be a good idea to make several copies of a checklist containing brief operating instructions and, most importantly, the locations of the items involved. Use this checklist when showing new crew members over your boat. On completion of the inspection and familiarisation tour, give the sheet to the person concerned so they can refer to it as required.

There are specialised books that go into these various safety aspects in great detail and my intention is to put you into the frame of mind, where you will accept that you must give safety your most serious consideration. The next step is to decide what gear and equipment is most suitable for your particular cruising needs.

With a couple of exceptions I have not included comments on the vast array of electronics available as support equipment for any boat. The technology used by these instruments is advancing at such a rate as to make any specific recommendations out of date before you could read my comments. Buying electronics is similar to purchasing a new computer; you think you have bought the most up-to-date and useful equipment until you have the opportunity to examine the following month's magazine devoted to that subject.

In a perfect world you should not have any item aboard your boat that you cannot repair or at least service properly. If you follow up on that thought then your array of electronics would be very small indeed. Choose the minimum amount of equipment you *must have*, hold off as long as you can before purchasing any particular item and then buy the best you can afford.

PROTECTION FROM LIGHTNING

This subject is far too complex for me to cover fully in the space available. I can offer some general advice, and alert you to the dangers of this potential killer. Lightning can be alarming at any time and it is certainly one of the most unnerving experiences you will have when cruising. It is comforting to know that most lightning damage is preventable. If you are in an all-metal boat then you can feel relatively safe because the boat acts as a Faraday cage and in the event of a lightning strike, the metal hull will divert the strike around the boat and into the water.

The best way to avoid damage from lightning strikes is to provide a path for the strike so it passes through your boat (or around it) and into the water. If you are unprepared and allow the strike to take its own path then it may destroy your electrical equipment and severely damage your hull. If your cruising boat is built of glassfibre or timber then you will need to have a 'bonding' arrangement so that the lightning strike is able to take a path to the water while at the same time bypassing your electrical equipment. 'Bonding' is the practice of connecting all large metal objects above and below decks such as tanks, engines, mast(s), rigging, life lines, pulpits and sail tracks, to a common ground plate. Connectors such as 6 AWG (16 mm²) cable or 4 in (100 mm) wide, heavy-gauge, copper strap will be required to carry the current to the metallic ground plate or strip that is fastened to the hull exterior below the waterline. The 'ground' allows the lightning to dissipate into the water after it reaches the plate via the system of connectors. Do not use the bonding system on metal boats.

Just as metal hulls offer a safety factor, when considering lightning protection, carbon fibre masts and hulls represent an additional danger. Carbon fibre is a 'noble' material and is a poor conductor. Electrical isolation of carbon fibre spars and hulls is necessary to protect them from the effects of a strike. Any laminate containing carbon fibre, no matter where it is used in the boat, is subject to severe damage from the excessive heat produced from a strike. In the case of the mast, you will need to ensure that a path, by way of a conductor cable, is provided both inside and outside the spar; this is in addition to the normal path arranged through the cap shroud/chain plate/ and on to the ground plate. Wooden masts will also need special attention by way of a conductor cable to provide a path from the top of the mast directly down to the ground plate.

Lightning dissipators are devices resembling a metal bottle brush and are mounted on the highest part of the vessel. The short bristle metal wires extend in all directions and operate on the principle that the numerous wires will dissipate the effects of the strike. These devices have a good track record and should be considered if your present or future cruising area is prone to storms that involve lightning activity. One device is known as the Lightning Master and is available from Forespar in the USA, see Appendix 3.

If you are caught in an area of lightning activity then the safest place is below decks; another good argument for a pilot house. Keep away from large metal objects and avoid touching metal and other items that may form a path for any strike. Remove any metal about your body including watches, ear rings, metal-framed eye glasses and chain jewellery. I know of one case where a boater who was wearing a gold neck chain was struck in the throat and killed.

It is a sad fact that, due to fear of litigation, some boat manufacturers do not install bonding arrangements in their boats. You should check if any protection has been built into your current or intended cruising boat. It should be possible to retro-fit adequate bonding arrangements as required. Additional information on protecting yourself and your boat from a lightning strike is available from several sources including the books *Boatowner's Wiring Manual* and *Boatowner's Mechnical and Electrical Manual*, see Appendix 2.

FIRE

An uncontrollable fire is one of the most devastating things that can happen on any boat. Once a fire really gets hold, there is very little you can do except abandon ship. You must avoid this situation by being fully prepared to extinguish any fire before it gets out of control. If all that sounds elementary then consider the following. Do you always introduce each new crew member (even those out for a day sail) to all of the safety aspects of your boat? Do you personally show all crew how to operate the safety devices including the fire extinguishers? If you feel that you are over-acting the captain-in-command routine by having safety drills before you set out on a short or long cruise, don't worry about it, your thoroughness may save someone's life, perhaps your own.

You will need at least one fire extinguisher for each compartment of the boat. In the average-sized cruiser this means a minimum of four units. Make sure these are in current service, check and log the expiry dates so that you either have them examined by the appropriate authority or refilled and/or replaced as necessary. Unfortunately it is not possible to test these units but do read and make sure you understand the instructions. Pass this information to all members of your current crew.

The two most likely places for a fire to start are in the galley and in the engine compartment. Give these areas special attention. Never leave a galley stove unattended; this is easier said than done, but make it a *strict rule* on your boat. Keep the galley clean and free from grease. Insist that rubbish and highly inflammable items are not allowed to accumulate in these areas and never store highly inflammable liquids in the galley.

A fire blanket is an essential item for every galley, make sure you have one and that it is stowed near the stove and in a location where it can be seen by all. When you are totally satisfied that the galley and engine space are as safe as possible check the rest of your boat for other areas that may present fire hazards.

Keep your engine compartment spotlessly clean. Regularly remove any build up of spilt fuel or oil; do not leave oily rags anywhere, and dispose of all items used as wipes, immediately after use.

Alarms and detectors

A smoke detector should be installed between the saloon and your sleeping cabin(s). Unfortunately, if you place the detector in or near the galley you will experience many false alarms so the unit must be placed elsewhere. When you are awake and on board you are unlikely to need a detector except in the engine room. If that area is isolated from the rest of the boat there are special alarms which are available to cover overheating and various types of gas leaks. Gas detectors are a must if you use bottled gas aboard your boat; choose your system carefully and make sure it is installed correctly and tested regularly. Burglar alarms are of limited value both ashore and afloat unless they monitored nearby. Today most burglar systems are based on motion detector and/or heat sensor technology. Unfortunately it is almost certain that you will experience so many false alarms as to make them almost worthless.

FLOODING

Equally devastating as fire on your boat is the presence of uncontrollable amounts of water. This hazard can enter your boat from several sources. Accidental holing of the hull, damaged inlet pipes and swamping are the most common causes of this problem. One interesting case involved a boat off the Queensland coast. This boat had black antifouling and it was attacked by a whale. There is some speculation that the whale thought the boat was actually a potential mate!

Examine your boat and make a list of the vulnerable points. Hopefully, your hull is strong enough to withstand a grounding, limited contact with rocks or a reef or unavoidable contact with whales and other marine mammals. The possibility of being sunk by a whale is no joke. There are many well documented cases where whales have actually attacked cruising yachts, so if possible, change course and stay out of their way.

Check hulls and seacocks

Make a careful assessment of your hull inlet fittings, stand pipes, underwater exhaust fittings, valves and hoses. Make sure every member of the crew is familiar with the locations of all these fittings. Renew any suspect items, double clamp all hoses and check all sea cocks; these should be turned off and on every month or so to make sure they do not freeze in one position.

Pay particular attention to any plastic through-hull fittings. The flanges can be destroyed by sunlight; use a scratch test to make sure the plastic has not deteriorated to the point of failure.

See if it is possible to reinforce areas where pipes enter and/or leave the hull. In glassfibre and timber hulls you may wish to laminate a round pad in place to thicken and stiffen the hull in the area of a skin fitting. In steel hulls, you may consider welding a similar piece in place using plate that is around 150 per cent of the thickness of the hull plating. Any hull thickening as suggested above, or for any other reason, should have the edges of the thicker portion chamfered to avoid creating a localised stress point.

You should have a bag of shaped, round timber plugs handy; you may need these to block off any inlet holes that have to be plugged in a hurry. Make sure you and the crew know the location of this collection of plugs, and better still, have one plug tied to each seacock so it is quickly available if needed. A collection of scrap timber, plywood, nails and glue could come in handy for making urgent repairs, not an excessive amount but a small selection of these items is recommended.

BILGE PUMPS

You should spend considerable time studying your bilge pumping systems. Bilge pumps can be electrically, mechanically or hand driven. Usually the first line of defence is the automatic, electrically-powered unit situated in the bilge. At least one of your bilge pumps should be situated in a 'strum' box. This is a special well in your bilge, created to hold a gauze covered end to the pipe that is in turn connected to the bilge pump. If you have an automatic shower pump-out system, this can double as another bilge pump; it will often be located in a different compartment to the main unit which is usually adjacent to, or in the engine space.

You will also need at least one, preferably two hand-operated bilge pumps; one of these should be a large capacity portable unit that is mounted on a board, thus allowing it to be operated in any area of the vessel. The Edson 18 and the Whale Titan are both excellent hand-operated pumps.

Many boats have a bilge pump that is driven by the main engine. A recent development that has come to my attention is the Ericson Safety Pump, a blindingly simple centrifugal pump. The Ericson unit has a harmonically balanced impeller that bolts to the propeller shaft on a boat. The unit is designed to be installed between the transmission coupling and the stuffing box. A loosely fitting pump housing covers the impeller. The suction port on the pump is simply a space between housing and impeller; the discharge port leads overboard through a hose.

Once installed, the pump operates whenever the boat's engine is running and the boat is in forward gear. In normal circumstances, of course, there will be no water around the propeller shaft, so the pump's impeller simply spins. Since the pump has no bearings, and there is no contact between the impeller and its housing, there is no wear. The only load on the engine is the minimal air resistance to the rotating impeller that will function as an engine room exhaust fan, sucking in air around the impeller, and discharging it outside.

FLOAT BAGS AND FOAM FLOTATION

I have always believed that float bags were a good idea but one that most of us would not consider because of the additional expense and some minor loss of stowage space. In their deflated form these bags, together with their individual, compressed-air bottles, take up very little room and are stowed in convenient areas of your boat's interior. In the event of serious flooding, the crew simply inflate the bags which more or less fill the interior of the boat and thus keep it afloat. The extra time gained can be used to make repairs or keep pumping out water until help can be summoned. A friend of mine, David Sinnett-Jones lost his 36 ft (11 m) *Zane Spray* off Ireland and had previously considered installing float bags but had not proceeded with the idea. As mentioned elsewhere, it is sometimes difficult to obtain comprehensive insurance for *long-distance* cruising boats and this makes the air bag flotation devices worth investigation (see Appendix 3).

There are a few boats that have been designed and subsequently built with sufficient foam flotion permanently installed to keep the boat upright and afloat in the event of flooding. Most of these arrangements only allow for enough flotion to keep the deck and superstructure just above the water; just a little better than being on a liferaft. The problem with foam flotation is that it takes up considerably more room than the deflated air bag. In most cruising boats, stowage space is at a premium so permanently installed foam flotation has not been exploited as a safety feature.

ABANDONING SHIP

Few of us have ever, and fortunately, will never, need to abandon ship. Only when there is a serious fire or the boat is actually sinking is it advisable to take to the liferaft. There have been many documented cases where crews have perished after abandoning boats which have later been recovered. The Fastnet Race of 1979 was a notable example. As I have no personal experience of abandoning ship, I recommend that you study the writings of *those that have*, see recommended reading in Appendix 2

Until recently there was not much educa-tion available to instruct in the art of survival in the event that you have to 'take to the boats' or in this case the liferaft. Fortunately several clubs and associations worldwide are giving this matter more serious consideration. In the UK the Royal Yachting Association (RYA) have made available a basic sea survival course. Do not be put off by the word 'basic', this course is highly commended by members of the RNLI and similar bodies. The RYA course starts with studying the equipment including lifejackets, survival gear and flares.

LIFEJACKETS

In the USA, lifejackets are graded as type 1 through to type 4.

Type 1 (offshore lifejacket), is recommended for use when help may be delayed; it has at least 22 lb (10 kg) of flotation and turns an unconscious wearer face up; it is bulky and difficult to swim in.

Type 2 (inshore lifejacket), is recommended when there is a chance of a quick rescue; and has at least 15.5 lb (7 kg) flotation; some models turn an unconscious wearer face up.

Types 3 and **4** have less buoyancy and I would not recommended these for use on cruising sailboats.

Australia, New Zealand and many other countries have their own rules for the manufacture and use of marine safety devices including lifejackets. When arriving in those countries in a foreign yacht, you could not reasonably be expected to have lifejackets that necessarily meet the local standards. You should ensure that these items meet the requirements of the country where your boat is registered and/or from where you start your cruise. New Zealand may be an exception; recently the authorities have insisted on inspecting boats before allowing cruises to continue. If New Zealand is on your list of expected ports of call you should check with the embassy regarding the current situation.

At some stage (hopefully before you ever leave port) you will take inventory of, or purchase lifejackets for all of the crew. Do not be impressed by the word 'lifejacket' which may be printed on the garment. Many items sold as lifejackets are really only flotation devices, these may be totally unsuitable for use in a serious emergency.

Buoyancy ratings

When you buy a lifejacket the most important factor is the buoyancy rating. Assuming the jackets you are considering are all brightly coloured and are equipped with whistle, reflective tape and a light, then the one with the highest buoyancy rating is the right one to buy.

In the EU there are several new rules covering the manufacture, sale and use of lifejackets. Here are the EU ratings and a brief explanation of their meanings. There are four categories of personal buoyancy device – all given a buoyancy rating in Newtons (N), with kg and lb equivalents.

50N buoyancy aid This is suitable for competent swimmers engaged in water sports in inshore waters where help is close at hand.

100N buoyancy aid (10 kg = 22 lb) In Europe they call this a lifejacket but it's not! It should only be sold for swimmers and for general inshore use. This type is not guaranteed to self-right an unconscious person wearing waterproof clothing or hold his airway clear in rough water.

150N lifejacket (16 kg = 33 lb) This is a standard lifejacket – suitable for swimmers and non-swimmers. For use in all but the most severe conditions. It will give a reasonable assurance of safety from drowning to someone not fully capable of helping themselves. However it may not immediately self-right an unconscious user wearing heavy waterproof clothing.

275N lifejacket (27 kg = 63 lb) A high performance lifejacket designed for working in severe conditions, when maximum protection is required or when heavy waterproof survival suits are worn. The 276N lifejacket will give improved assurance of safety from drowning to people unable to help themselves. It is not *guaranteed* to right an unconscious person in heavy gear, but it will in most cases.

Since July 1995, manufacturers have sold only lifejackets and buoyancy aids which have been tested to the new European specifications and carry the CE mark. Look for this label which will clearly show how much buoyancy the approved garment contains. There's no legal requirement for sailors to replace serviceable lifejackets which they already own.

Foam-filled lifejackets

The advantage of this lifejacket is that the buoyancy is always there, there is little to go wrong and this type is usually cheaper to buy. Their disadvantage is that they are bulky and cumbersome to wear, so are only used in real emergencies and don't tend to be worn as often as they should be. Like any lifejacket, they're not much use in the locker!

Inflatable lifejackets

These require minimal stowage space, and are comfortable and unobtrusive to wear. When attached to a waterproof jacket you forget about them – so they're often worn while sailing. Their disadvantage is that you have to trust that they'll work in an emergency. Automatic ones have been known to burst due to faults in the material. Lifejackets which have been stored in the bottom of wet lockers have been rendered inoperative with trigger mechanisms so corroded as to be useless.

There are three different types of inflation:

Oral This type is economical to buy but you must inflate it before going into the water. Inflation when you're swimming is very difficult.

Manual gas inflation Probably the most popular because it will only inflate when you trigger. Remember that this is not much good if you fall in unconscious!

Automatic gas inflation These should inflate within five seconds of hitting the water. They're popular with many yachtsmen, especially those who are weak or non-swimmers or suffer from epilepsy. The disadvantage is that they can deploy unintentionally, if you get swamped by a wave while working on the foredeck. It is worth noting that the RNLI don't wear them in their RIBs because in the event of a capsize they'd inflate and trap the wearer under the boat. Air-foam lifejackets are a compromise between the two basic types and for that reason are fairly popular.

Special features

There are a few beneficial features to look for when purchasing new lifejackets: retro-reflective tape, a whistle (this is much more effective than shouting), and lifting becket to help to pull the casualty out of the water. Each jacket should be fitted with a light (manual or automatic); you will find lights are standard on commercial jackets so purchase these if you cannot otherwise find ones fitted with a light. Another feature worth looking for is a combination safety harness which toggles on to a sailing jacket. Leg and crotch straps are seldom worn, but they make a huge difference when in the water. Commercial jackets have additional features that you may find desirable including a hood that reduces the chance of drowning by breathing in spray, and also two separate inflation and buoyancy chambers. Like most things, there will be a compromise between what you'd like and what you can afford!

Make sure everyone in your crew is familiar with your particular type of lifejacket. Practise putting it on. Make sure all of the crew, including new arrivals, are shown where the lifejackets are located; because these items are not often (hopefully never) required, they tend to be stowed in less desirable stowage spaces.

LIFERAFTS

A liferaft is an essential piece of equipment for any cruising boat. When it comes to choosing one there are several different approaches you can take. Firstly, you may decide that by obtaining a Tinker inflatable lifeboat you will have the best of all worlds. The Tinker, which is made in the UK, is obtainable throughout the world and has become a popular alternative to a traditional liferaft. The Tinker brand inflatable dinghy can be fitted with sails and makes an excellent dinghy which can be used for ferrying stores, yourself and crew to and from shore. You may have to remember to restock it as a lifeboat after it has been used for trips and shopping.

Traditional liferafts come packed in one of three basic cases. The valise is the lighter alternative and needs to be packed in a waterproof locker; if not kept dry, then salt water will soon attack your flares, torch and inflation gas cylinder. This type of packaging is usually favoured by the racing set. A vacuum-packed valise has been developed to overcome some of the problems mentioned above; a unit packed in this way usually only needs servicing every three years.

The third and most often seen option is the canister-packed liferaft which graces the cabin tops and transoms of many cruising boats. Because of the cost of the canister itself, these units are generally more expensive than the valise-packed liferafts. These units are designed to be exposed to the elements and so do not take up valuable locker space. You will need to check where the drain holes are located in your unit as some can be stowed vertically while others will need special packing to allow them to be mounted in that way. One of the drawbacks of the canister-packed liferaft is that its exposed position on deck increases its vulnerability to theft.

Liferaft types

There are various types of liferaft each designed for a different purpose; not only are the rafts different but the emergency equipment and contents vary depending on the intended use for the raft.

The basic inshore or coastal raft is usually built to a price and there are many models available at this lower end of the market. These units usually only have a single buoyancy chamber and often do not have an inflatable support for the canopy. In my opinion these so called liferafts are only one step up from a regular inflatable dinghy.

The RORC is one of the most popular types and if you add the emergency pack (referred to as the E pack) of equipment and emergency provisions you will have a satisfactory unit at an affordable price. Your liferaft should contain paddles, hand-held red flares, parachute rocket flares, signalling mirror, fishing kit, water, food, first aid kit and a bailer.

If you want a very well equipped raft then you could add the following items (before the raft is packed): multi-purpose knife, sea anchor and spare, raft repair kit, anti-seasick pills, signal card, scissors, graduated cup, radar reflector and, most importantly, a reverse osmosis desalinator. This latter item will produce about a cup of fresh water from seawater by pumping, in about 15 minutes. An alternative is to have these additional items form part of your 'grab bag' package. There are many other things you may *like* to have with you when you are out in the middle of an ocean in your liferaft but remember you have to fit yourselves in without overloading the raft.

Grab bag

Your grab bag will contain your valuable small possessions such as passports, credit cards, ship's papers, extra water and food, plus other items that you feel will be essential in the event you have to abandon ship in a hurry. Remember to include appropriate quantities of any prescription medicines required by yourself and your crew, including children. Remember that the grab bag may be needed not only for transferring to the liferaft, but also when being transferred to another vessel or helicopter; keep this in mind when preparing your bag.

SAFETY LINES

Safety harnesses and jack lines should be rigged to the decks and superstructure so the crew can *clip on* when moving around the boat. Make sure these lines have secure anchoring points and are arranged so they do not form a hazard to trip up unwary crew. Make sure that you and all the crew are familiar with the hook-on arrangements; use only tested devices. There have been many well publicised instances where the snap shackle or other clip-on arrangements have failed under load. Be warned and only purchase the best quality items of this sort.

MAN OVERBOARD AND PERSONAL RECOVERY DEVICES

It is imperative that you practise 'man overboard' drill as soon as practical after you have acquired your boat. Check that you have liferings and other recovery devices in place and that you know how to use them.

You should consider purchasing one of the special slings that are available for recovering a person from the water. As it is often very difficult to assist a rescued person back on board (even if you do get a line to them), you should have a pre-assembled device, similar to a sling made from sail cloth or netting that can be slipped under a person and used to hoist them back on board.

Practise the recovery procedure using this item but after taking precautions such as having the 'victim' wearing a lifejacket. Make sure that the dinghy is launched and then only allow this practice to take place in temperate water. At all times stow your recovery sling where it can be quickly brought into service and most importantly, advise all the crew of its whereabouts. (For suppliers see Appendix 3.)

RADAR REFLECTORS

For your own safety you must have one of these devices aboard and in many countries they are mandatory. There are several types including the traditional metal diamond-shaped version that can be stored flat and then assembled when you go to sea. Remember that this type must be hung in the 'rain catching' position and not by the top of the diamond. Metal hulled boats have an advantage here; they present a better image on a ship's radar screen.

EMERGENCY STEERING

As well as carefully checking over your steering arrangements you must have some form of emergency steering that has already been tested *before* you go far offshore. The emergency tiller is the simplest and best method of arranging alternative steering. The simplest tiller arrangement is to have the top end of the rudder shaft squared off to take a tiller with matching squared-off fitting to quickly slip over the shaft. The tiller may have a pipe extension and a hatch above the rudder shaft location (to allow you to see out) or a deck fitting to allow the passage of the tiller extension will be required. Some accommodation arrangements will make it more difficult

Slings like the one pictured here can be purchased from Morlasco or you can make your own device.

to arrange this necessary feature but as emergency steering is essential, you must plan ahead.

EPIRB

These letters stand for Emergency Position Indicating Radio Beacon and they work in much the same way as the emergency locator transmitters that have been standard equipment aboard aircraft for many years. When activated, the EPIRB devices are programmed to send out a signal on a VHF channel that is monitored by shipping and aircraft, and many sailors have been rescued due to their plight being registered by a ship, aircraft or shore station. Unfortunately these regular EPIRB signals are in a crowded area and not always monitored, for safety's sake you should seriously consider the COMPAS/SARSAT.

COMPAS/SARSAT is a newer version of the EPIRB that operates on 406 Mhz. It is designed to take advantage of the latest satellite technology and has superior operating accuracy to the regular EPIRB. These new systems are expensive but as with all electronic devices the prices should soon start to come down to an affordable level. These devices are mandatory in some countries.

PERSONAL SAFETY ABROAD

Laws and social conventions vary considerable from country to country, so for trouble-free cruising, the wise sailor will do plenty of research on the legal requirements and customs prevailing in the countries he or she intends to visit. (See Appendix 2 for useful reference books.)

Firearms

The decision whether to carry a gun on your cruising boat may have already been decided on your behalf; for example, if you are already or intending to cruise in UK waters it is definitely not recommended. There are many other countries where the carrying of even one gun on your boat would bring you grief when it was either declared or discovered by the local authorities. Quite frankly, your decision may be influenced by your views on owning and using firearms. About 30 years ago I owned a .22 rifle, but as I was such an appalling shot and could not hit anything I sold the weapon and have never had the desire to own another. If you fit a similar profile my advice is do not change the habits of a lifetime. Even if you are familiar with firearms and an excellent shot, you may be well advised to leave your guns at home.

Ask yourself this question: if you do take a gun on your boat when you go cruising, would you be capable of using it against another human being? If you think the answer is yes, remember that the only way to be sure of making effective use of a gun is to shoot first! I doubt whether that would be your decision when the occasion arose. However this can still lead you into trouble. Recently there was a report in the yachting press that illustrated tragic misuse of a gun. A cruising sailor in the Greek islands was awakened by noises on his deck; he made enough noise from below to frighten off the intruders, and made his way on deck in time to see them piling into their dinghy and motoring off. However, he went below and retrieved his gun and fired a couple of shots in the general direction of the retreating intruders; they replied with automatic rifle fire and the yachtsman was killed. It is reasonable to assume that if 'you keep your head down' you stand a better chance of surviving any robbery or similar event. Also if you are carrying guns there is the possibility that thieves could find your weapons and use them against you and your crew.

Smuggling

What is smuggling? You had better hope that you do not find out the exact interpretation of this term in some foreign place. In some countries you will need to declare any 'trade goods' before you start swapping them for local produce. As the rules vary from country to country (from customs officer to customs officer) you will need to be careful that you do not fall foul of local officialdom. Perhaps the best advice is not to carry any materials aboard your boat which could be regarded as surplus to your needs. I doubt that personal clothing, food supplies, spares for your engine and normal cruising gear and equipment in explainable quantities would get you into trouble. Carefully check rules and regulations before you trade with the locals.

In some countries in the Middle East and elsewhere, the possession of pornographic materials can get you into severe trouble. Many years ago I knew a cruising yachtsman who always carried a good stock of *Playboy* magazine aboard his boat for the express purpose of trading these with locals on the Pacific islands (at least that is what he told me). Well the world has changed considerably in the last 25 years and today it is not advisable to carry any article, picture, video or other material that could be considered pornographic, blasphemous or otherwise offensive to other cultures especially in countries you expect to visit.

Dress code

When you are considering your cruising wardrobe you must keep in mind that what may seem perfectly normal in our own country may give offence and threaten your personal safety in others. In many areas women and to a lesser extent men are expected to observe a modest dress code that we would find unusual. Those of you who have travelled as tourists to foreign parts will already have a good sense of how to dress. To avoid problems when visiting a country where the local women dress 'modestly', follow their example to the extent that you cover up limbs and shoulders. Men do not escape these conventions, in some areas brief shorts or going bare chested can offend, so study local dress customs before you shed your clothing.

CHAPTER 11

Medical Emergencies and First Aid Kits

◆ *Forms and paperwork* ◆ *Medical kits* ◆ *What to carry for medical emergencies* ◆ *Safe sun* ◆ *Books on first aid*

There are no medical emergency or casualty departments at sea. Even when conveniently close to shore you will find that the facilities that are taken for granted at home are often not available in areas where you may be cruising. The time for planning the medical care for yourself and your crew is before you leave your home port.

FORMS AND PAPERWORK

If you require medical attention in neighbouring countries, you will need to make provision for this occurrence *in advance*. UK residents when cruising in EU waters should have an E111 certificate for each member of the crew; this will ensure that they are entitled to medical care in any EU member state. Non-EU residents can obtain care under the National Health Service when in the UK especially if they are sponsored by a UK resident.

Those venturing outside the EU or not wanting to rely on the facilities of member states, should consider expatriate medical and health insurance such as provided under BUPA and similar organisations. EU residents be warned that the medical insurance rates for the USA and Canada are usually twice the cost of the same cover for the rest of the world. You may be able to obtain a short term 'holiday insurance' cover for the period that you are in North American waters.

Residents of the USA, Australia and many other countries who intend to cruise in Europe and even further afield, may find it worthwhile to investigate the availability of UK-based medical insurance to cover serious emergencies.

FIRST AID TRAINING

If you plan to undertake coastal or even canal cruising, you still may find yourself in a location where you have to depend on your own resources to deal with a medical emergency that may involve yourself or your crew. At least one member of your crew should therefore undertake an advanced course on first aid. One source of such training is the St John Ambulance Brigade which is a worldwide organisation and has immense experience of training people to deal with medical emergencies.

MEDICAL KITS

You will need to carry a medical kit but hopefully you will not need the type of package that was reported in the UK magazine *Yachting World*. Lynne Oakerbee wrote that when the Department of Transport's Code of Practice for small commercial vessels was applied to the letter (remember that word). A small example of what was required would include: a body bag (large), 1000 aspirins (one adviser suggested that they would need six body bags if they took all of those aspirins on their short cruise to the Mediterranean). Listed as an 'optional extra' were 72 condoms, quite a large number for a crew of six during a two-week delivery voyage. The Yacht Charter Association suggested that they would need to tow another boat behind to carry all the medical supplies and equipment specified. After a considerable discussion with the DoT, a revised list was supplied (still including the body bag) but, thankfully, this list was only *nine* pages long.

Many of the first aid kits advertised in mail order catalogues or available in department stores contain a minimum variety of dressings and plasters and not much else. Do not be fooled by the red cross insignia, this is no guarantee that the first aid kit will meet your needs. You will need a much more comprehensive medical kit at sea.

Fortunately there are specialised companies which make up kits for boats. When selecting your kit you should consider your special requirements. Where will you cruise? What type of protection will you need from the local insects etc? How many crew are you likely to have aboard at any one time and what are the premedical conditions that may require special attention? The foregoing is in addition to planning for the normal run of cuts, scratches and burns, that are all too easy to acquire in a boat that often will be moving in several directions at the one time. You must be able to offer assistance in any medical emergency that may arise in your cruising boat.

The Royal Yachting Association's cruising guide *Yacht Safety: Sail and Power* points out that unless a patient is bleeding profusely, unconscious or not breathing, they will usually survive an accident, even if you do nothing. Notwithstanding these comments, I believe that for your peace of mind and to inspire confidence as well as to relieve pain it is wise to be prepared with the right knowledge and medical kit.

As a minimum, your medical kit should contain items to treat the following: severe pain, coughs, sea sickness, wounds (including infected wounds), burns (including scalds and sunburn), allergic reactions to insect bites and stings, diarrhoea, constipation, hangovers, splinters, athlete's foot and conjunctivitis.

BASIC MEDICAL SUPPLIES

- 50 assorted adhesive plasters, including waterproof, fabric, heel and finger types.
- Quantity of sterile dressings: 20 non-stick type (10 cm x 10 cm), 10 No8 or 13BPC type, 2 No9 or 14BPC type, 2 extra large (28 cm x 18 cm), 2 gauze pads with attachments and 10 paraffin gauze type.
- Assorted bandages: 2 crepe type (75 mm), 2 sterile gauze type (50 mm), 2 triangular type (90 cm x 127 cm).
- 6 rolls of adhesive waterproof elastic strapping (7.5 cm x 5 m).
- 2 rolls of adhesive medical tape (2.5 cm x 5 m).
- 1 pack of adhesive suture strips.
- 2 packs of sterile cotton wool (15 g) and 1 pack of cotton buds.
- 30 antiseptic wipes plus solution (500 ml) and cream (50 g tube) and disinfectant (500 ml).
- 1 burn bag (31 cm x 46 cm)
- 2 eyepads, including 1 with headband.
- 1 pack of finger dressings and applicator.
- 1 mouth-to-mouth resuscitation mask.
- 2 packets of aspirin, ibuprofen or paracetamol painkillers (500 mg), syrup version for children (100 ml).
- 1 jar petroleum jelly (225 g).

- 6 medium rustless safety pins, 2 splints, 10 pairs disposable gloves.
- 1 measuring spoon.
- 2 forceps, stainless steel with pointed ends for splinters and plastic with rounded ends for dressings.
- 1 pair 18 cm scissors with one blade sharp pointed and the other end rounded.
- 1 strip type or stubby-bulb thermometer.
- 1 waterproof torch.
- 1 notepad and pencil for noting casualty's symptoms and treatment.
- 2 dental first aid kits, including filling material, swabs, mirror and spatula.
- 1 emergency medical kit for use by doctor or nurse, including 2 syringes (5 ml), 5 needles, intravenous canula, dental needle, skin suture and needle, skin closure strips, alcohol swabs, non-stick dressings (5 cm x 5 cm and 10 cm x 10 cm) and roll of surgical tape, all sterilised where applicable.
- 1 first aid manual (see Appendix 2) or as published by St John Ambulance or Red Cross Society.
- 1 waterproof protective case, with bulkhead mounting if possible.
- Plus extra requirements for specific medical conditions

If you prefer to make up your own medical kit (you may have to do this in any case due to your special requirements), rather than purchase a ready-packed version, most of the essential items can be obtained from any pharmacy without prescription. Add your special needs to this list and make sure that all are packed in a moisture-proof container in such a way as to be easily identified and readily accessible when required in a hurry. Whenever possible keep your medical kit up to date, keep a check on the 'use by dates' especially in the case of medications that are to be taken internally.

SAFE SUN

The effects of too much exposure to the sun's rays are not immediately apparent and often the problems only surface after many years. Some of us are paying the price for exposure that we enjoyed some 20 years ago or as children. We are told now that the sun can be more damaging to our health than in the past, due to a hole in the ozone layer; in any case all cruising folk should practise 'safe sun' exposure. The UV element that forms part of the sun's rays is one of the most damaging components; fortunately avoiding these harmful rays need not detract from the cruising experience. In Australia children and adults alike are advised to 'slip, slop, slap and wrap', slip on a shirt, slop on sun screen, slap on a hat and wrap on those sun glasses. This is good advice, no matter where the sun is shining.

Sunburn is not only painful but in cases of severe burning it can leave effects that will not become manifest for some years. It is not good enough to apply a sun tanning preparation of unknown factor to your exposed areas and believe you have all the protection you need. Most sun creams now clearly show the factor of protection on a scale ranging between 2 and 35. If you are unaccustomed to being in strong sunshine then choose water resistant sun screen with a factor of 15 or more.

People with fair skin or with a history of sun-induced skin problems need to cover up. It is recommended that they wear clothing that has been made from cloth that has been specially formulated to screen out UV rays. In any case, this sounds like a good idea. Fortunately, attractive Lycra-based garments are now available that will offer up to 100 per cent protection; check the label for UPF ratings. In hotter climates, your headgear should have a cloth at the rear and sides as well as a forward facing peak to give you all round protection in these areas.

Constant and prolonged exposure to strong sunlight can damage your eyes. It is not commonly known but you can develop a serious condition called pterygium which is an opaque tissue that develops over the cornea of the eyes. This condition has shown up mainly among surf board riders and others who have had constant and prolonged exposure to sun, wind and salt water. All of this reinforces the need for good quality sunglasses; the versions with polarised lenses not only protect your eyes but make it much easier to pick out underwater obstructions. If you normally wear eyeglasses for reading or to correct your long distance vision or both, then it will be worth investing in sunglasses that have optically corrected lenses to suit your requirements. Select sunglasses that offer side protection; the effect of the sun getting in behind your glasses can be as damaging to your eyes as the effects of direct sunlight.

Make sure you have a proper safety device such as a neck cord to keep the glasses on your person; I recently saw an expensive pair of my bifocal sun glasses disappear into the depths when I failed to heed my wife's advice to use a safety cord. This is a good time to remind you to take at least one spare pair of glasses with you when you go cruising; imagine being the navigator when you have lost your only pair of reading glasses!

Even if you reside in a cool climate and have not given much thought to 'sun proofing' your boat, a few days in one of the hotter cruising areas will soon convince you that some shade protection is urgently needed. Cockpit awnings and cloth hatch covers are a standard requirement in sunny climes; however blinds and side awnings are also needed to shade large pilot house windows. Make sure your cockpit awning is fitted with battens so that it can be tilted from one side to the other; this will enable you to avoid the sun from either side. This arrangement has the additional benefit of shading the cockpit from slanting rain. Remember to make up covers for your instrument panel and individual covers for the various instruments that are located where the sun can reach them for even a few hours each day. Modern navigational and other electronic instruments are not resistant to heat and strong sunlight so keep them covered when not in use.

The *siesta* practised in many of the countries with the hottest climates is not a sign of lethargy, but rather a sensible cultural development that has a very practical benefit. When at sea, the siesta may not be a practical consideration but excessive sunbathing by members of the off-watch crew should be discouraged. When in port try to plan excursions ashore during the mornings and evenings and avoid exposure when the sun can cause the most damage.

Tinted windows not only look attractive and provide some privacy when in port, they also keep out some of the sun's harmful UV rays. Laminated glass containing a layer of special plastic is available and this glass will stop virtually all UV rays. It is worth checking on the properties of the glass or glazing plastic that you are considering, as the UV screening values will vary. For existing windows you may elect to add a self-adhesive film, similar to those used in cars and existing buildings. Check that the type of film, you choose is suitable for application over the surface of your windows; some plastics need special semi-permeable film. Make sure that the film can be removed without the use of harmful solvents.

FIRST AID BOOKS

There are several books and publications available advising on the treatment of accidents and illnesses when professional help is unavailable. At least one (or preferably more) of these books should be purchased and thoroughly read before the medical emergency arises. The Royal Ocean Racing Club recommends the book *First Aid At Sea* co-written by Dr Douglas Justins and Dr Colin Berry. Dr Justins has extensive cruising experience including sailing non-stop from Sydney to Dover and competing in the Fastnet race. Dr Berry is an anaesthetist and has completed two circumnavigations and served as a medical officer in the Royal Navy.

Another one of the most frequently recommended books is *First Aid Afloat* by Dr Rob Haworth. The writer of this book has vast experience in dealing with medical emergencies on small craft and holds a RNLI silver medal for bravery. Even if we cannot have the good doctor on board our boats, we can have his book, which includes a wealth of information. The pages of *First Aid Afloat* contain step-by-step guidance for novices including what action to take in the event of a medical accident or health emergency happening on board your vessel.

As well as listing various types of medical kit, these books recommend that the skipper should be made aware of any premedical condition of any crew member so that additional medical supplies are carried for special emergencies. Remember that prescriptions that are easily filled at home may not be so easy to obtain in a foreign port. If anyone has a special medical condition, make sure they have adequate supplies of the prescribed drugs to last for the length of the voyage. It is a good idea for the labelling on all prescription drugs to be very clear and include the ship's or owner's name. In the case of drugs needed by a particular crew member for an existing condition, the label should include the patient's name. The above precautions may make it easier to explain the presence of certain drugs aboard your vessel if you encounter a over-zealous customs official.

CHAPTER 12

Choosing the Crew

◆ *Partnerships* ◆ *Charter guests* ◆ *Casual crew*

It is an old saying that 'an unhappy crew makes for an unhappy ship'. The confined spaces in even a moderate sized boat will soon bring out the worst in many people, so choosing who shares your cruise will be one of your most important decisions. It is also said 'that you can choose your friends, but not your family'. If, in this case, the family are your own children, then the considerations are quite different to those that exist if you are planning to take other relatives along. For the purposes of deciding who will accompany you for all or part of your cruising, it may be better to judge these other family members as friends. Do they measure up in this respect?

Before you take anyone cruising, you must spend some time with them ashore, under similar conditions to those you will experience on your boat. During the preparation stages, you may be able to all get away together. Choose the type of holiday where you will be in close company and preferably under some stress. If you already have acquired your boat, then short cruises are one way to see how you all react, and interact under these conditions.

INTIMATE PARTNERSHIPS

Strange as it seems today, I can remember a time when two people of the opposite sex could not book a double cabin on a passenger liner unless they were legally married. Married or unmarried, you must make sure that your relationship is well tested in other areas before you take off on a long-distance cruise. There are literally thousands of happy couples currently cruising in various parts of the world. A number of these relationships do falter, mainly due to the lack of planning and the understanding of just what is involved in *long-distance* cruising. If you are the 'prime mover' in this adventure, then you should introduce your partner to the experience *gently* and over a reasonable period, before you take off on a round-the-world cruise.

During this early period, choose your weather carefully and do not attempt to impress your partner by sailing in conditions where prudent

sailors have already reached shelter. Act macho and your cruising dreams will surely founder before you can leave home waters. After you have studied your partner's reactions to various experiences and weather conditions, it may be time to start to explore wider horizons. If one or both of you enjoy coastal and local cruising and you do not want to venture further afield, take heart, for you represent the greater number of happy cruising couples.

Maureen Jenkins had no problems in choosing her crew; she sails her boat single-handed and recently was the only Spray owner to arrive at the Azores on the same day as Slocum did exactly 100 years ealier.

FINANCIAL PARTNERSHIPS

On occasion you may want to consider a boat partnership, usually with another couple and perhaps occasionally with another family. As designers, we are often approached to prepare plans for cruising boats that could comfortably accommodate either two couples, or in some cases two families. In our experience, the best partnerships appear to be those where the partners use the boat at different times.

Some arrangements consist of two partners where one has more time and less capital and the other has the capital but can only make infrequent use of the boat. An example of this arrangement could be that Partner A provides half (or more) of the capital to purchase the boat and provides half of the cost of replacement parts. Partner A uses the boat for a limited number of weeks during the most desirable part of the season. Partner B puts up half the original cost (or less) and pays for half the cost of replacement costs but partner B personally undertakes all of the maintenance work on the boat. Partner B makes sure that when his partner gets to use the boat it is in a desirable location and is ready and in pristine condition. This arrangement has worked out well for some owners and could be regarded by partner A as owning a boat complete with an unpaid maintenance crew.

One notable partnership was between Peter Campbell who is an experienced professional skipper/boatbuilder and a Californian doctor. Peter supplied the labour to build a 40 ft (12.2 m) cruising boat, the doctor supplied the materials. Peter had the use of the boat for a set period of years and in that time sailed from California to Australia and later back to the USA, then it was the doctor's turn to use the boat for the same period. Years later I met Peter Campbell who, by this time, was captain of a bulk carrier; he told me the arrangement worked out well for both parties. I must add that considerable faith and safeguards would need to be involved in an arrangement such as this; the success in this case reflects favourably on the characters of the parties involved.

The largest number of partners who to my knowledge have shared a boat was five male school teachers, who shared their building and cruising experience while jointly owning one boat. In this case it worked fine until some of them met various ladies and eventually married. Eventually one partner bought out all of the others, but all appeared happy with their joint ownership experience. I am personally aware of many two and three single-person partnerships where the owners did cruise (some around the world) together for many months at a time. The partnerships were successfully concluded when one or more of the individuals left to marry or continue a career.

There are obvious financial advantages of sharing the costs of obtaining and later operating a sailing boat. You will know if you are the type of person that can be involved in a successful partnership. If you are convinced that the other parties share your ability to get on with others in difficult situations, this option is worth your serious consideration. Make sure you have a written and legal agreement covering all the foreseen eventualities.

CHARTER GUESTS

You may be fortunate enough to know personally, people who have crewed on or operated a charter boat. Make use of their intimate knowledge on how to deal with paying or non-paying guests aboard your boat. If you decide to accept charter guests regularly, then your opportunities for personal choice of crew will become more limited. Most likely you will

have charter guests who will have booked through an agency. You can hardly refuse to accept the guests, who are waiting dockside to join your boat, simply because you do not like their looks.

Many owners find this Roberts 53 design ideal for use in the charter business.

When planning regular charter activities you will need to decide in advance just how you will go about finding your clients, what method you can use to vet them against your preferences and how and when to say no. These days, for example, it should not be a problem to ban smoking from below decks. Smoking in the bunk was always a non-starter and should be treated with the same seriousness as when passengers are caught smoking in aircraft toilet compartments. There are now many non-smokers who object to the smell and other residues of smoking, as well as the thick atmosphere of a smoke-filled cabin. You should have no problems in insisting that smoking activities take place on deck, and preferably downwind of other crew members.

If you are a non-smoker yourself you may want to consider banning smoking on your boat altogether; perhaps non-smoking charter parties would work to your advantage. A boat that has never been smoked in will have a different aroma to one that has even occasionally hosted a heavy smoker. All of this may bring benefits, similar to those enjoyed by non-smoking hotel rooms, non-smoking flights, etc.

CASUAL CREW

It is a dangerous practice to pick up casual crew from the dock. When you give it some thought you could compare this with stopping by the roadside and picking up a hitch-hiker in the dead of night. Once you have left port with an unknown crew on board you cannot get rid of them until you make the next port. Make it a rule to never accept a new crew member unless they are already personally known to yourself or are recommended by a trusted friend or family member.

So far I have mainly been thinking of the *dangers* involved in accepting unknown crew members. You may be lucky and just end up with a person with distasteful personal habits! To be fair, there are only a few recorded instances where an unknown crew member has inflicted bodily harm on the owner and family. However, the potential for problems is enormous, so take care.

CHAPTER 13

Cruising with Children and Pets

◆ *Safety aspects* ◆ *Catering for children's needs* ◆ *Taking your pet along* ◆ *Legal problems*

Many couples take their children cruising; in fact sometimes one meets a family where the children have never lived ashore. Having youngsters on board will require making provision for their comfort, welfare and safety. Even if you only have them aboard occasionally you will need to make some changes and the new arrangements will extend to every part of the vessel. Babies and very small children generally are easiest to care for on a boat; they usually stay where you place them. Toddlers are another matter! It is usually more dangerous having guest toddlers on board than it is to have your own continuously with you on the boat. Your older children will become 'boat wise' and may not need supervision 24 hours a day. Your medical kit will need special attention and revision – child's dosages of various non-prescription medicines will need to be included. Make sure your 'grab bag' contains any quantities of any special prescription medicines and any other items that relate to the safety and welfare of your children. If you are planning to have children on board then you will find useful information in the book *Cruising with children* by Gwenda Cornell, see Appendix 2.

SAFETY ABOVE DECKS

On deck, the usual set-up to safeguard youngsters is to arrange netting all around the lifelines as well as pulpit and pushpit areas. Safety lines should be rigged so a child can be hooked on, not only at sea, but in the case of small children, in port as well. When a small child is on deck it is essential that they be under the supervision of an adult *at all times*. Only parents know just how quickly a child can make some unexpected move that will take them into danger in a matter of seconds. Obstructions that an adult would naturally step over may present a hazard to a child; check your deck and cabin top areas to see if these can be made less hazardous. When

This Mauritius 43 was built in the centre of Australia and trucked 500 miles to the sea. Note the safety netting around the lifelines but closer-spaced netting would be safer.

considering the special arrangements you will need to make on deck, this is also a good time to review your 'person overboard' recovery arrangements. (see Chapter 10).

Children must wear life jackets at all times when they are not below decks; to be effective, the jackets must be a suitable size for the children wearing them. Parents and all grandparents (after the first visit) will be very aware of how important it is to 'child proof' their home; in a boat the importance of taking safety measures cannot be over-emphasised.

SAFETY BELOW DECKS

Below decks you must ensure that stoves and other areas where children can harm themselves are protected so as to avoid accidents. Never leave an operational galley stove unattended, make sure it is impossible for a child to burn, scald or otherwise be harmed in or around the galley area. Throughout the boat the availability of extra handholds are essential at *the child's level*. Steps or a raised sole area will need to be provided in the heads to enable a young child to reach the hand basin and toilet. You may want to consider a safety strap as part of the toilet arrangement to prevent the child from being thrown about in rough seas. A lee cloth is essential on children's berths; and a good idea for your own as well. Depending on the layout of the interior, the steps and stairs may need special attention.

CHILDREN'S SOCIAL ACTIVITIES

If your children are at the age where they have friends that they would like to bring aboard for a short cruise, this can be a positive rather than a negative experience. Firstly, it will help amuse your own children to have a friend aboard; they will enjoy showing off their knowledge and teaching the young guest how to perform the tasks they have already learnt. Let your children and their occasional guests bring some of their own entertainment gear aboard. Personal stereos, cameras, favourite games and other items that do not conflict with life aboard will go a long way to keeping the younger members of your crew amused and more eager to continue to cruise with you in the future.

Sometimes your children's friends can bring a new perspective to a cruise; for instance on one occasion the teenage daughters of a client of mine, took along a school friend who was interested in astronomy. The three children slept on deck for several nights studying the night sky and discussing the stars and much else! The parents were able to enjoy some unexpected privacy which went a long way to extending their enjoyment of this particular cruise.

Providing you take the usual safety measures, you will find that the ship's dinghy will provide safe and enjoyable entertainment for the children. If your boat is large enough you may consider carrying an extra dinghy which can be the children's responsibility. This can be another way to involve the younger crew members and turning the cruising experience into a truly family affair.

PROVISIONING FOR CHILDREN

Provisioning arrangements will need to be modified especially if you have children aboard other than your own. Let your hair down and give the collective children a handful of cash and send them off to the supermarket to purchase items other than the basic staples. As a parent you will have more control over what your child consumes when you are cruising, but it is wise to allow for this by being a little more flexible than you would be ashore. Birthdays and similar anniversaries take on a special meaning especially if they occur during a long sea passage. Make sure you have considered these coming events when you are provisioning your boat.

TAKING YOUR PET CRUISING

Many of the cruising arrangements needed for the safety and consideration of children are also needed when you take your pet along. Placing netting around the perimeter of the decks, providing a secure sleeping space; these and other arrangements will be similar to those you would arrange at home. It is well to consider that should your pet be left unattended to wander at will, the results may be more disastrous than those encountered on dry land. You will need to consider how you will go about keeping your pet amused; allowing for the uniqueness of the new location, similar methods to those employed at home will probably work best.

Various types of pets involve special and individual arrangements for their care and welfare; for instance there is a vast difference in looking after the interests of a small cat versus a large dog aboard any cruising boat. The toilet arrangements that you make for your pet at home may need to be modified to make them acceptable to the confines of a boat. In the case of a cat which is the most popular pet found aboard a cruising boat, you must consider where the 'kitty litter' tray will be located. Dogs are a little more difficult to toilet train but it may be possible to modify your dog's social behaviour in this manner, otherwise you will have to resign yourself to 'picking up' after your pet. Depending on the species of your pet, you may find that the additional provisioning is either difficult or in some cases downright impossible. My advice is that you should only consider taking your pet(s) on short weekend or holiday cruises. However, it is a fact that in some families there will be times when certain members of the family will not want to go if the pet is not included.

It would be nice to have a guard dog aboard but you will need to decide if the disadvantages outweigh the benefits. Perhaps certain types of reptiles may be considered as part of the boat's security system!

Legal problems

It is well known that one cannot import or re-import most pets into the UK; what is less known is that many other countries have restrictions on the movements of pets. For instance when two American friends of mine cruised to Australia they had two parrots on board; whilst in that country, the customs authorities insisted that the parrots be kept below decks at all times. The rub came when they decided to sell their boat in Australia. They had many problems before they were able to import the birds back into the USA. Before you take any pet cruising, make sure you check on the relevant laws in your own country as well as those in the countries you are likely to visit.

CHAPTER 14

Summary – A Designer's Perspective

◆ *What makes a good cruising sailing boat?* ◆ *Opinions of a designer and cruising yachtsman*

The earlier chapters of this book have been written to give you an overview of the features that are needed to make a true cruising boat. This boat can be used in local waters, for coastal cruising or for crossing the world's oceans. In all cases the boat will share several features not found in many of the boats at your local marina. In this summary I would like to express my personal opinion as a designer and cruising yachtsman.

THE DESIGN PROCESS

Over the past 30 years there have been great advances in cruising boat design. This does not mean that the older designs are no longer worth your consideration, simply that now you have a wider selection to choose from than ever before. Most cruising boats are developed rather than designed from scratch. All established naval architects' offices contain a collection of existing designs. The data collected as these designs are built and tested, is used to refine existing designs and develop new ones. Very few designers start 'with a clean sheet of paper' when preparing a new plan. The process usually starts when a client approaches the design office and states something like this: 'I like your XYZ design but I would like it longer, shorter, shallower or with a different accommodation layout' or incorporating any one of many other changes.

If these modifications can be incorporated into the existing design without changing any of the basic fabric or essential elements of the boat, then this may be termed a *semi-custom* design. If the changes are such that the basic concept is altered, or if there are several changes, then this usually results in a full custom design which is given a new name or other special designation and a new design is born.

CHOOSE THE RIGHT DISPLACEMENT

All cruising boats, no matter if they are intended for local or extended cruising, have to carry considerable amounts of weight. It is no use considering very light displacement sailboats; they are just not up to the job. No matter what the brochure says, when loaded (as a cruising boat must be), these boats cease to be light displacement. Overloading any boat will destroy its potential performance; *overloading a light displacement boat can be disastrous*. In other words choose the range of displacement suitable for your intended usage. If you intend to go either local, coastal or round-the-world cruising, choose a boat with a *designed* displacement that is up to the job.

HULL MATERIAL

When choosing a hull material my preference is for steel, or finance permitting, the hull would be built of steel and the decks and superstructure would be built of aluminium. If you visit many of the world's popular cruising anchorages you will find that around one-third of the boats are all steel or have steel hulls. If you visit your local marina and examine the rows of boats many of which rarely leave their moorings, then you will find a preponderance of glass fibre boats. This does not mean that glass fibre boats are not suitable for cruising, it simply means that many experienced crews have decided that steel-hulled boats are best suited to their needs. Many of the cruising fraternity whom I have met in person show a clear preference for steel; and some who currently own boats built of other materials intend to make a change when acquiring their next boat.

KEEL TYPE

This is a simple choice; for myself I prefer a long keel. Here I am considering two examples of long keels; one is a type seen on very traditional designs including the Spray and the other is the modern 'long keel' that has been developed over the past 30 years. Either of these two long keels, when combined with the correct hull form offer many advantages.

My second choice would be a moderately long fin keel combined with an adequate skeg and fence combination. This arrangement offers good directional stability and excellent manoeuvrability but it does need to be strongly built. I would rule out having the propeller located in an aperture created in both the skeg and the rudder. This combination deprives the prop of free water and structurally weakens the skeg as well as detracting from the performance of the rudder. If you are having a keel/skeg fence configuration then equip your boat with a good 'rope cutter' and install it just ahead of the propeller.

Among my favourite designs, the Roberts 34 is one of over 800 built (including a sister ship Northsea 34) which was sailed three times singlehanded around the world by UK yachtsman Leslie Powles.

THE RIG

As mentioned earlier, the choice of rig will be a matter of matching the rig to the boat and injecting some personal choice. My opinion which is backed up by discussing this matter with hundreds of cruising sailors is as follows: cruising boats under 30 ft (9 m) can be rigged as Bermudan sloops (although some owners still prefer a cutter rig). Boats of around 40 ft (12.2 m) LOD are best rigged as Bermudan cutters. Boats over 52 ft (15.8 m) are best rigged as Bermudan cutter-headed ketches. In between 40 ft (12.2 m) and 52 ft (15.8 m)it is a matter of personal choice.

The suggested size-breaks between single-masted cutters and twin-masted ketches is not only based on the ease of handling for the typical two-person crew, it takes into account the way the sizes of masts, rigging and sails affect the costs. For instance it is often less expensive to rig a large sailboat as a ketch than as a single-masted cutter; this is especially true when considering boats over 60 ft (18.3 m). It is a fact that off-the-shelf deck hardware and fittings for the larger boats are becoming more readily available; it was only a few years ago that much of the equipment required by a 53 ft (16.2 m) sailing boat had to be custom made at great expense. Today the range of ready-made equipment is slowly sliding upwards in size; unfortunately the costs move upwards at a far greater rate.

Raising and lowering the mast(s) on your cruiser is something you should consider when you are selecting your boat. Broadly speaking the larger the boat, the more difficult you will find the mast raising operation without outside assistance. The inclusion of a substantial mast tabernacle will be a consideration for boats of up to around 40 ft (12.2 m); gaff-rigged boats with their relatively shorter masts are better able to take advantage of this feature.

For myself, what type of rig would I choose for our next cruising sailboat? Serious consideration will be given to using a junk or lug rig (same thing). In my opinion this rig is easily handled by a cruising couple, is less expensive to install and maintain and the spars can be shaped from natural grown trees. There is no standing rigging to purchase or maintain and a well-designed rig offers better than satisfactory performance on all points of sail. Finally the junk rig has a charm all of its own, as they say: beauty is in the eye of the beholder!

WHAT SIZE OF BOAT?

The above brings us back to considering what size of boat is the most practical. If you are a single person or a couple and this is your first boat and you plan to cruise rather than use the boat for day or weekend sailing, then you should consider 25 ft (7.6 m) LOD as the minimum. I consider 28 ft (8.5 m) as the minimum size for a cruising boat, but I know many people who have happily cruised in smaller boats, and so I bow to their experience when quoting 25 ft (7.6 m). I also know of people undertaking long cruises in very small boats; however if you have the choice then it is better to start

This glass fibre version of a Mauritius 43 was built in 1972 and is another of my favourite designs. The pilot or dog house is designed so that if the structure is damaged, the remainder of the boat remains intact and free from flooding.

with a reasonable size. My personal opinion is choose as big a boat as you can *comfortably* afford, up to a maximum of 45 ft (13.7 m)

Next, let us consider a long-distance cruising boat or a boat which you intend to use as a full time live-aboard. A boat of about 38 ft (11.6 m) is affordable and can be arranged as the perfect boat for two. If you seriously plan to carry additional crew or have a family of four, in my opinion 43–45 ft (13–13.7 m) is the correct length. These size recommendations do not take into account waterline length; depending on the DWL, any of these boats can be either small or large for their given length on deck (LOD).

If you are planning local cruising or wish to use your boat for charter, then you may be expected to consider sizes below or above those suggested above. Please note that the sizes mentioned here are not just my opinion: they also reflect the opinions of literally thousands of cruising people that I have met in the past 30 years.

If you cannot afford (or do not want to gamble) so much of your savings to reach the optimum size of boat do not despair; more importantly, never make yourself *boat poor*. Cruising is meant to be fun and if you cannot afford to enjoy your chosen lifestyle, you will soon tire of the whole exercise.

COCKPIT LOCATION

Aft or centre cockpit, that is the question! If a pilot house is to be included in the design then I prefer an aft cockpit configuration. It is a desirable feature to be able to walk directly out of the pilot house and into the cockpit without having to climb or descend steps. This feature is the nearest I am ever likely to get to the lifestyle enjoyed by the owners of large power cruisers who can stroll from the large saloon out on to the spacious aft deck *avec cocktail*, and deposit themselves in one of the comfortable chairs ever so casually located for their pleasure.

A centre cockpit configuration allows a designer to make the best use of the available space in boats around 40 ft (12.2 m) and larger; this together with the apparent security this feature provides makes this an option we always offer in larger cruising sail boats.

ACCOMMODATION

My choices in this area are somewhat influenced by lifestyle; I *know* that 90 per cent of my time on board will be spent with the boat securely anchored or in some foreign port. It is a fact that most cruisers including full-time live aboard sailors spend the greater portion of their time snug in some harbour. As we mature, so our values change; in my case to enjoy boating fully, I need more comforts than in previous years.

My present boat has a individual shower, totally separate from the head compartment. This fully-tiled area doubles as a drying room and wet

locker depending on the weather and our location. On-demand pressure hot water is also a nice luxury and one that I would not like to relinquish. At present we have a forced-air diesel-powered heating system; next time, I would choose one or more diesel-fuelled, drip-feed heaters. The latter are much easier to keep operational.

Seating on my next boat will be designed around two really comfortable chairs. All seat backs need to have enough lean-back to provide a comfort-

This centre cockpit Roberts 43 was originally designed in 1969. Over 1000 have been built in glass fibre, steel and wood/epoxy and cruised world wide.

able posture. On the sole I prefer carpet, this can take the form of removable rugs that are used when in port or fully-fitted carpet.

THE AUXILIARY ENGINE

An adequately sized *diesel* auxiliary is a must aboard any cruising boat. The diesel engine must be located where it is easy to service, but where it can be sound-proofed so that when in operation, it does not intrude on your quality of life. Can you hold a normal conversation in the saloon, pilot house or cockpit when the engine is running? For me, this is the test any engine must pass. Two horse power per 1000 lb (2 hp per 454 kg) displacement is about right; diesels like to be worked so don't grossly overpower your boat in the belief that your engine will last longer. The worst treatment you can give a diesel is to run it for long periods at idle speed; this 'glazes the bore' and shortens its life.

IN CONCLUSION

It is a fact that choosing a cruising boat is a question of personal preferences. All I have tried to do throughout this text is to provide enough information to enable you to make informed choices. Those of you who are so inclined, please feel free to contact me via the US or UK Bruce Roberts Design offices and I will be pleased to offer you such personal advice as is appropriate to your situation (see Appendix 3).

CHAPTER 15

Why not Choose Inland Cruising?

◆ *Equipment for inland waterways* ◆ *Cruising Dutch canals*
◆ *Belgium* ◆ *French waterways*

If you are just starting to think about cruising as a holiday recreation, or you would just like a change of pace, I recommend that you consider inland cruising which has a lot to offer.

EQUIPMENT FOR INLAND WATERWAYS

To cruise canals successfully a boat must have a selection of equipment that may not be so relevant for regular offshore sailing. Additional fenders and mooring lines are an absolute necessity. The mast needs to be supported in timber cradles at the bow and stern, and arranged with minimum over-hangs at each end. Other necessary equipment includes two steel jerry-cans to carry spare diesel fuel, a long hose and assorted fittings, a plastic container for carrying water (in some areas canal-side taps are in short supply), engine spares, gangway/mooring plank, searchlight for the tunnels, air horn, mooring spikes and a set of courtesy flags for each country you plan to traverse.

CRUISING DUTCH CANALS

In Holland paperwork is kept to a minimum. For boats of under 49 ft 3 in (15 m) in length, and whose top speed is less than 8 knots (15 km), all that is required is a recognised form of operator's certificate such as the International Certificate of Competence issued in the UK by the RYA. As with any cruise, the requirements may change so you should always check with the local authorities of each country you plan to visit. Make sure you are equipped with the correct ship's papers, local guides and rule books before you leave your home port. In Holland you are required to purchase a copy of the Dutch ANWB book and strip maps. Although the text is in Dutch, they will prove most useful. These along with other guides can be purchased from Shepparton Swan in the UK (see address in Appendix 3).

A proven offshore cruiser *K*I*S*S* was until recently owned by the author. With a draft of 3 ft 6 in (1.1 m) and an air draft of 7 ft 9 in (2.4 m) she is ideally suited to canal cruising; here she is pictured with her new owner Ian Crosfield.

As some of the locks (*sluizen*) are multi-chamber affairs, it is essential to have a VHF radio available to call up and ask advice as to which is the next available lock. Make sure you let the lock keeper know if you are travelling upstream or downstream.

Many towns in Holland levy a charge of about 10 Guilders (£4 sterling or US$6) for an overnight mooring at the bollards laid out by the town. Facilities vary; rubbish bins and drinking water are usually available.

Crossing the turbulent Amsterdam Rinjh Canal and the river Waal (a lower section of the Rhine) requires a vigilant look-out. Huge barges and small ships approach from both directions at alarming speeds, creating unbelievable amounts of wash. There is only one rule when dealing with barges and large shipping: keep out of their way. Many of the locks in Holland are big enough to give one a taste of what is to come, and the experience of sharing them with several large barges will stand you in good stead when dealing with the locks throughout Belgium and France.

BELGIUM

On arrival in the French-speaking area of Belgium, you have to pay 35 BFr (about 75p or US$1.20) for using the canal system. The modest fee is offset by the fact that one of the crew will have to climb up to the office at every lock to have the 35 BFr piece of paper stamped and recorded on the computer or occasionally entered into a log by hand. In the Flemish areas to the north the fees are considerably higher.

Heading south you now enter the Meuse river that runs between Maastricht, Liege and Givet. Before crossing into France you can take the last opportunity to fuel up with the tax free, and therefore much cheaper, Belgian diesel fuel. On crossing the border you are now able to use the excellent French Navicarte maps which have English, French and German text; the various editions cover the entire French canal system. The maps show every lock (*ecluse*), including details of size, VHF channel numbers, distance between locks and details of canal side towns as well as features of general and historical interest.The availability of rubbish disposal, fuel and water supplies is clearly indicated. Some editions have a photograph of each bridge indicating which arch to pass under or how to approach a tricky lock entrance. Costing about £10 sterling (US$16) per issue, these maps are essential.

FRENCH WATERWAYS

At the first lock inside France and before reaching Givet, you must purchase a *vignette*, the permit for the French canal system. At this lock, leaflets explaining the various permits are available in English, Dutch and German. There are different options such as a 15-day pass designed for holiday makers and must be used on 15 consecutive days, a 30-day pass, which can be used as you wish, you do not count the days you are not actually travelling on the canals, or a one-year pass for those who plan to be on the move for more than 30 days.

Most foreign canal users choose a 30-day *vignette* costing 900 FFr, (about £100 sterling or US$160). Run on the honour system, the *vignette* allows you to mark off the days as you use them, but this is backed up by the lock masters who occasionally ask you for the vessel's name and record this information on their computer. Heavy fines are enforced on those who try and cheat this practical arrangement. Usually there is no frequent request for examination of the ship's papers. Throughout France you can expect to be treated with courtesy and friendliness at all times. You are required to have another booklet *Vagnon Carte de Plaisance* obtainable from the RYA. The *vignette* is also obtainable in advance (see useful addresses Appendix 3).

The canalised sections of the river Meuse between Givet and Corre are known as the Canal de l'Est (Nord), and the *Carte Guide No 26* covers this section. The locks in this area are smaller, generally 126 ft (38.5 m) long by 16 ft 6 in (5 m) wide so this restricts the size of barge you are likely to encounter. There are several tunnels in the French canal system and most have traffic light systems, as do the locks and opening bridges. Never ignore these lights, or you may have to make a very quick about turn when a large barge appears around a blind bend in a narrow channel.

At least 50 per cent of the locks are controlled by keepers; the rest are automatic and operated by a variety of methods. In some cases you are supplied with an electronic box the size of a cigarette packet which you point at a receiver located on a pole about half a mile (1 km) before the locks and this registers your passing and prepares the lock. In some cases a long sausage device hangs over the centre of the canal and you give this a twist to operate the locks. There are fail-safe systems built into these arrangements, so you need never fear that you will become stuck in a lock gate.

Sometimes in mountainous areas, the locks are quite close together, some only a half mile (1 km) apart; in these cases you can cover as many as 35 locks in one day, but you may have travelled only 15 miles (24 km). Other days when the locks are spaced further apart you may travel up to 75 miles (125 km). Do not tow your dinghy, this is bad practice and can cause problems when you are locking through and is a nuisance to others using the same lock.

Bois l'Abbe is the highest point, and after 15 closely spaced locks, life becomes easier. For those heading south this is the end of the 'up' locks and the remainder including those on the mighty Rhône river will be the 'down' variety; down locks are less turbulent and easier to use. The next section is on the Saône which, in its canalised form, is known as the Canal de l'Est (Sud) and runs from Corre to Lyon. This 230 mile (370 km) stretch has only 24 locks and it is easy to cover an average of about 70 miles (113 km) per day.

Located midway in this stretch is St Jean le Losne, where the intersection of three canals prompted the canal authorities to dig out a large basin where commercial barges used to spend the winter. With the decline in barge traffic, this area has been turned into marinas, and the largest of these, H2O, is operated by two expatriates one English and the other German (Robert Bond and Charls Gérard), who have created a popular meeting place for all canal cruisers. There is no shortage of social life on the canals.

The River Rhône has long been the bogeyman of the French canal system. Even though the Rhône has been tamed, it still holds a fearsome reputation, especially if one is unlucky enough to encounter one of the local mistral winds which can blow on rare occasions at over 100 miles per hour (160 km). Fortunately most mistrals are less fierce and reliable up-to-date weather information is available at either end of the Rhône. It is possible to cover the 170 mile (274 km) section between Lyon, and the turn off at Arles, in two and a half days. The scarcity of overnight stops will spur you on and the favourable current will add an extra one or two knots to your true speed.

The locks on the Rhône are the largest in France and the Ecluse Bollène is over 80 ft deep (24.4 m) and large enough to take most ocean liners. It is advisable to call the Rhône locks on your VHF radio to advise of your impending arrival; this can save you up to two hours' delay if you just miss

the lock cycle. With a few phrases spoken in French you will greatly enhance the chances of the lock master holding the cycle for up to 15 minutes or more, when others are already in the chamber. The right time to call ahead depends on your speed. If you call from too far out you may be holding up the lock for too long and annoy the lock keeper (not recommended). Most canal users find that calling when about 10 to 15 minutes from the estimated arrival time is correct. If the lock keeper does not reply, leave it for a few minutes and try again, he may be handling a lock full of barges and be unable to get to the radio. You must supply the correct information in French if you want this useful system to work in your favour. Turn on your radio, select the correct channel and the VHF conversation goes something like this:

'*Allo, Ecluse Bollène*' (example), '*Ecoutez-moi*' (Hello, lock Bollène, do you hear me).

Usually the reply comes promptly and as the keeper realises you are not a fluent French speaker the reply will most likely be '*Bonjour, je vous ecoute*' (Good day, I hear you), so far so good.

Now the keeper needs to know in which direction you are travelling, from up or down stream, what are you, are you a large barge or a pleasure boat, and how many minutes are you from arriving at the lock. So take a deep breath and refer to your prepared speech: '*Bonjour, Je suis montant(upstream)/avalant (downstream). Je suis un bâteau privè. J' arrive*

This medium-sized lock can take many barges and pleasure boats at one time; pay attention to your boat handling or you will incur the wrath of the busy lock keeper.

en quinze minutes' (Good day, I am upstream/downstream. I am a pleasure boat. I will arrive in 15 minutes).

The lock-keeper will most likely respond with *'Je prepare l' ecluse pour vous'* (I am preparing the lock for you) or *'L' ecluse est pret'* (The lock is ready) or *'Attendez vingt minutes'* (please wait for 20 minutes). Now unless you are fluent in French, and even if you did not understand the reply, turn off your VHF as you can achieve no more at this stage.

When you reach the lock you will be able to appraise the situation and act accordingly. Most of the larger locks have a tannoy hailer system and the keepers may instruct you where they want you to moor. In locks where there is a gate in the centre, only half the lock will be used for smaller craft, always proceed to the forward chamber; no need to go right up to the end lock gate, as that can be where there is more turbulence.

During your trip down the Rhône a convenient overnight stop is at Avignon. You can find a well run marina near the bridge made famous in the French folk song. The remainder of your trip consists of a day's run to Arles and then you must decide whether to turn off into the Petite Rhône and the Canal Rhône a Sète and on to the Canal du Midi, or turn right to Port St Louis and out into the Mediterranean.

If you are not in a hurry, take your time as there is much to see and enjoy. You can easily travel from Holland, Belgium or from one of the French channel ports to the Mediterranean in 18 days; a leisurely trip through France can take a whole summer or two!

Appendices

APPENDIX 1

Equalizing Batteries

BY MAX PILLIE

◆ *Information specific to Heart Interface 'Link' chargers is given here however much of the advice will be helpful when using any charger to equalize your batteries.*

EQUALIZING BATTERIES

Equalizing or conditioning batteries refers to a method of charging deep cycle, wet cell batteries which is intended to restore battery capacity, revive battery efficiency and extend battery life. The process involves periodically applying a controlled overcharge cycle to batteries. This type of charge cycle requires that certain procedures and precautions be followed.

WHY EQUALIZE BATTERIES?

While a battery is being discharged, sulphuric acid in the electrolyte reacts with the lead plates in a chemical reaction which produces electricity and lead sulphate. When the battery is recharged, electricity flows back into the battery and causes a reverse chemical reaction which turns the lead sulphate back into lead and sulphuric acid. However with each discharge and recharge cycle, a small amount of lead sulphate will remain on the plates. Using a three-stage charger will minimize the amount of residue and sulphate left on the plates but some will still accumulate with each discharge and recharge cycle

If this sulphate is left in place for very long, it will harden or crystallize and eventually reduce the battery's capacity, increase its internal resistance and destroy its ability to produce an adequate amount of power. When this occurs, even an equalizing charge cannot remove the sulphate and the battery becomes useless except as an item to be recycled to reclaim the lead and prevent contamination of the environment.

Also, in time, the electrolyte tends to stratify into layers of acid and water with higher concentrations of acid near the bottom of each cell and more diluted electrolyte near the top. This causes uneven *specific* gravity within a cell, further reducing its capacity and efficiency.

THE EQUALIZING PROCESS

An equalizing charge is a controlled overcharging cycle which performs several actions within the battery and provides certain benefits. During equalizing the voltage is raised to approximately 2.7 volts per cell, or about 16.2 volts for a 12 volt battery The current output of the charger should be limited to about 50 per cent of the battery's capacity. In other words, a 200 amp hour battery should be allowed to accept no more than about 10 amps of current. This will help prevent overheating. The equalizing cycle is timed to be between four and eight hours depending on the features of the charging source but the cycle can always be terminated early if necessary. The particular battery manufacturer's recommendations for equalization time should be followed.

This elevated voltage results in a vigorous charging action taking place within each cell which has several effects on the battery. First, much of the residual sulphate is forced to recombine with the electrolyte in the form of sulphuric acid. Crystallized sulphate which will not recombine is broken loose from the plates and falls harmlessly to the bottom of the battery. Deep-cycle batteries have additional space beneath the plates intended to collect this material. This action cleans the plates exposing fresh lead to the electrolyte and restores battery capacity.

The vigorous bubbling action which occurs during equalization stirs up the electrolyte and restores it to a consistent mixture of acid and water. The equalizing process also causes all cells in a battery to reach their maximum idle potential of 2.1 volts.

WHEN TO EQUALIZE

It is best to check with the battery manufacturer's recommendations before equalizing. Each manufacturer has slightly different suggestions on how often and how long to equalize their batteries. But, as a general rule, it is a good practice to equalize batteries after every 10 or 12 deep discharge and recharge cycles. For batteries in constant discharge and recharge usage this would mean about every two weeks. For periodic users, it would mean about two or three times a year. For seasonal users this could mean at the beginning and end of the season. When using a battery monitor such as a Link 2000, equalizing should be done when you notice the charge efficiency factor (CEF) begin to drop.

HOW TO EQUALIZE

Check with the battery manufacturer's recommendations but, as a general rule, the following steps should be observed:

1 Only attempt to equalize wet cell, deep-cycle batteries. Never equalize gel batteries or maintenance free batteries.
2 The batteries should be fully charged and near ambient temperature before beginning an equalize charging cycle.

3   There should a sufficient amount of electrolyte in each coil to cover the plates, but do not top up each cell until after equalizing Since there is some heating of the cells during equalization, the electrolyte will expand and could overflow the cells if they were topped up before equalizing. This would not only make a mess, but force you to terminate the equalize cycle too early to gain maximum benefit and would result in diluted electrolyte when it was time to add water.

4   Leave the caps on each cell. The caps are vented and, when left in place, will prevent splattering of electrolyte on to the top of the battery when the bubbles pop. It is a good idea to lay a paper towel over the caps. This makes it easier to spot a cell that may start to spit electrolyte, and the towel will soak up the liquid when this does happen.

5   Since the batteries will give off significant quantities of explosive hydrogen and oxygen gas during equalizing, and produce moisture which will contain some amount of corrosive sulphuric acid, it is imperative that sufficient ventilation be provided. Avoid smoking or generating any sparks or flame near the batteries during this charge cycle.

6   All DC loads on the batteries should be turned off and disconnected. Since the battery voltage will be higher then normal during this charge cycle, some DC equipment could be damaged if left on. Also these loads would draw current from the charger which should be available to the battery instead.

7   Equalize only one bank of batteries at a time.

8   With older Freedom inverter/chargers, to limit the charging current to less than 15 amps DC, set the power-sharing feature of the charger to 5 amps AC using the remote control panel. Newer versions automatically set a special equalizing current limit during the equalizing cycle.

9   During the equalizing cycle, periodically check batteries for any spitting cells. If this begins to happen, terminate the equalizing cycle early. Never start an equalizing cycle and then leave the batteries unattended.

10   After equalizing, turn off the charging source, and allow the batteries to cool to ambient temperature before resuming normal float charging. After the batteries cool it is a good time to check the specific gravity in each cell. They should all be 1.265 +/- .050 at 80° F, 26°C.

11   Refill each cell with distilled water up to the full indicator.

START/STOP EQUALIZING CHARGE CYCLE

When using the standard Freedom remote control panel, an equalizing charge cycle is started by turning dip switch #1 on for one second and then back off again. This will start an 8-hour equalizing cycle. After the cycle time is complete, the charger will go to float mode. To terminate the cycle early or to allow the battery to cool down after equalizing, AC input power to the charger should be interrupted. When AC power is reapplied to the charger it will resume normal charging.

When using the Link 2000 remote control panel start the equalizing charge cycle by first turning ON the charger and waiting until it goes into the float mode. Then press the SET UP button and hold it until it begins to flash. Then release the SET UP buttons and immediately press both the VOLTS and AHRS (amp hours) buttons simultaneously and hold for five seconds until the red CHARGE LED begins to flash and the E in the display goes out. To terminate the equalizing cycle, always force the charger into the float mode, repeating the same set up procedure. The cycle will automatically terminate after 8 hours or if AC input power to the charger is interrupted.

When using the Link 2000R to control equalizing using the Freedom charger, it will operate the same as the Link 2000 described above. If the alternator is the charging source, some differences will be apparent. The procedure for start/stop equalizing is the same, but the control of the charging source (alternator) is different. The cycle is 3.5 hours long and the charge current is limited to 4 per cent of battery capacity up to 16 amps maximum.

ADDITIONAL PRECAUTIONS

If some cells in a battery begin spitting electrolyte during equalizing and continue spitting long after the charger has been turned off, this indicates that the spilling battery may have a shorted cell. If this happens, disconnect any batteries which are in parallel with the questionable battery as these batteries will continue to supply current to the questionable battery and cause it to get very hot. When it cools down, check the suspect battery with a hydrometer. A shorted cell will read much lower than the others. If this is the case, the battery must be replaced. Batteries which are likely to develop a shorted cell are more likely to do so during an equalizing cycle, since the buttery is being subjected to more thermal stress during this type of charge then it is accustomed to. The chances are that the battery could have developed the shorted cell sooner or later anyway but it's better to find this out when the batteries are being closely monitored as during an equalizing cycle.

Whenever working with batteries, always wear protective clothing and eye protection. Avoid generating sparks, open flame or smoking near batteries.

Recommended Reading

PILOTS AND CRUISING GUIDES

Adlard Coles Pilot Packs, Brian Goulder, Adlard Coles Nautical (UK)

Atlantic Pilot Atlas, 2nd Ed, James Clarke, Adlard Coles Nautical (UK)

Atlantic Cruising Guide, 3rd Ed, RCC Pilotage Foundation, Editor: Ann Hammick, Adlard Coles Nautical (UK)

Brittany and Channel Islands Cruising Guide, David Jefferson, Adlard Coles Nautical (UK), Sheridan House (USA)

Cruising Guide to the Caribbean, Michael Marshall, Adlard Coles Nautical (UK)

Cruising Guide to the Caribbean, William T Stone and Anne M Hays, Sheridan House (USA)

Cruising Guide to the Tennessee River and Tenn-Tom Waterway, International Marine (USA)

Mediterranean Sailing, Rod Heikell, Adlard Coles Nautical (UK), Sheridan House (USA)

Normandy and Channel Islands Pilot, 9th Ed, Mark Brackenbury, Adlard Coles Nautical (UK), Sheridan House (USA)

North Biscay Pilot, 4th Ed, RCC Pilotage Foundation, Editor N E Heath, Adlard Coles Nautical (UK), Sheridan House (USA)

Norwegian Cruising Guide, 2nd Ed, John Armitage and Mark Brackenbury, Adlard Coles Nautical (UK), Sheridan House (USA)

Pacific Crossing Guide, 4th Ed, Editor Michael Pocock, Adlard Coles Nautical (UK), Sheridan House (USA)

Paris by Boat, David Jefferson, Adlard Coles Nautical (UK)

Planning a Foreign Cruise, Vols I and II, Cruising Association/RYA (UK)

Quimby's Cruising Guide, Waterways Journal (USA)

South Biscay Pilot, 4th Ed, Robin Brandon, Adlard Coles Nautical (UK), Sheridan House (USA)

Slow Boat Through Germany, Hugh McKnight, Adlard Coles Nautical (UK), Sheridan House (USA)

Tenn-Tom Nitty Gritty Cruising Guide, Cruise Guide (USA)

The European Waterways, Marian Martin, Adlard Coles Nautical (UK), Sheridan House (USA)

Through the French Canals, 8th Ed, Philip Bristow, Adlard Coles Nautical (UK), Sheridan House (USA)

Through the Dutch and Belgian Canals, Philip Bristow, Adlard Coles Nautical (UK), Sheridan House (USA)

Through the German Waterways, Philip Bristow, Adlard Coles Nautical (UK), Sheridan House (USA)

Turkey and the Dodecanese Cruising Pilot, Robin Petherbridge, Adlard Coles Nautical (UK), Sheridan House (USA)

Vetus Marina Guides: Mediterranean and Netherlands, Vetus (UK)

Waypoint Directory: English Channel, Peter Cumberlidge, Adlard Coles Nautical (UK)

World Cruising Handbook, 2nd Ed, Jimmy Cornell, Adlard Coles Nautical (UK)

World Cruising Routes, 2nd Ed, Jimmy Cornell, Adlard Coles Nautical (UK)

GENERAL CRUISING TITLES

Cruising with Children, Gwenda Cornell, Adlard Coles Nautical (UK), Sheridan House (USA)

Cruising: A manual for Small Cruiser Sailing 4th Ed, D J Sleightholme, Adlard Coles Nautical (UK), Sheridan House (USA)

Cruising under Sail, Eric Hiscock, Adlard Coles Nautical (UK)

First Aid at Sea, 2nd Ed, Douglas Justins and Colin Berry, Adlard Coles Nautical (UK), Sheridan House (USA)

First Aid Afloat, Dr Rob Haworth, Fernhurst Books (UK)

Handbook of Offshore Cruising, Jim Howard, Adlard Coles Nautical UK), Sheridan House (USA)

Sailing Alone Around the World, Joshua Slocum, Sheridan House (USA), Adlard Coles Nautical (UK)

Sail into the Sunset, Bill and Laurel Cooper, Adlard Coles Nautical (UK), Sheridan House (USA)

Sea Survival – A Manual, Dougal Robertson (UK)

Sell Up and Sail, Bill and Laurel Cooper, Adlard Coles Nautical(UK), Sheridan House (USA)

Spray, the Ultimate Cruising Boat, Bruce Roberts-Goodson, Adlard Coles Nautical (UK) Sheridan House (USA)

Survive the Savage Sea, Dougal Robertson (UK), Sheridan House (USA)

117 days adrift, Maurice and Maralyn Bailey Adlard Coles Nautical (UK), Sheridan House (USA)

BOAT MAINTENANCE

Boatowner's Mechanical and Electrical Manual, Nigel Caulder, Adlard Coles Nautical (UK), International Marine/McGraw-Hill (USA)

Boatowner's Wiring Manual, Charles Wing, International Marine/McGraw-Hill (USA) Adlard Coles Nautical (UK)

Boatbuilding, Bruce Roberts-Goodson, Capall Bann Publishing (UK), Bruce Roberts (USA)

Metal Boats, Bruce Roberts-Goodson, Capall Bann Publishing (UK), Bruce Roberts (USA)

Modern Boat Maintenance, Editor Bo Streiffert, Adlard Coles Nautical (UK), Sheridan House (USA)

The Care and Repair of Small Marine Diesels, Chris Thompson, Adlard Coles Nautical (UK), Sheridan House (USA)

APPENDIX 3

Equipment Manufacturers and Useful Names and Addresses

DESIGN/CONSTRUCTION

ABYC (American Boat and Yacht Council)
Construction standards for small craft
3069 Solomons Island Road, Edgewater MD 21307 USA
Telephone 1 410 956 1050
Fax 1 410 956 2737

Bruce Roberts Designs (UK)
Cruising boat plans and custom designs
Orchards, School Lane, Easton, near Woodbridge
Suffolk IP13 0ES UK
Telephone 44 (0)1728 747 427
Fax 44 (0) 1728 747 663

Bruce Roberts Designs (USA)
Cruising boat plans and custom designs
PO Box 1086 Severna Park MD 21146 USA
Telephone + 1 410 268 4611
Fax + 1 410 268 4612

ENGINES/PARTS

De Bug TM (USA)
Micro-organism fuel filters
Environmental Solutions International
11002 Racoon Ridge, Reston VA 22091 USA
Telephone 1 800 411 3284
Fax 1 703 620 2815

Halyard Marine Ltd (UK)
HMI Shaft seal, exhaust systems, engine insulation
Whaddon Business Park, Southampton Rd, Whaddon, Nr Salisbury SP5 3HF UK
Telephone 44 (0)1722 710 922
Fax 44 (0)710 975

Lancing Marine (UK)
Marine diesel engines and rebuild kits, etc
51 Victoria Rd, Portslade
Sussex BN41 1XY UK
Telephone 44 (0) 1273 410025
Fax 44 (0) 1273 430 290

Southwester Ltd (UK)
Deep Sea Seals and other marine gear
Stinsford Rd, Poole
Dorset BH17 7EU UK
Telephone 44 (0) 1202 667 700
Fax 44 (0) 668 585

Vetus Den Ouden (UK)
All types of marine equipment, gen sets, engines, fuel and water tanks, ventilators, etc
38 South Hampshire Industrial Park, Totton, Southampton, Hants SO40 3SA UK
Telephone 44 (0)1703 861 033
Fax 44 (0)1703 663 142

Vetus Den Ouden (Holland)
Fokkerstraat 571 3125 BD Schiedam, Holland
Telephone 31 10 437 7700
Fax 31 10 415 2634

Vetus Den Ouden (USA)
PO Box 8712 Baltimore MD 21240 USA
Telephone 1 410 712 0740
Fax 1 410 712 0985

ELECTRICAL EQUIPMENT

Apollo (USA)
12 V and 120 V generating sets
833 West 17th St, No 3, Costa Mesa Ca 92627 USA
Telephone 1 714 650 1240
Fax 1 714 650 2519

Cruising Equipment Company (USA)
E-Meter and other battery monitoring devices and services
315 Seaview Ave, NW Seattle WA 9807 USA
Fax 1 206 782 4336

Exide Batteries Ltd (UK)
Marine batteries
Gate no. 3, Pontselyn Industrial Estate,
Pontypool, NP4 5DG UK
Telephone 44 (0) 1495 750 075

Heart Interface Corporation (USA)
Battery chargers, inverters and battery monitors
21440 68th Avenue South, Kent
WA 98032 USA
Fax 1 206 872 3412

HFL Industrial and Marine Ltd (UK)
AC Generating sets
HFL House, Lockfield Ave,
Enfield Middlesex EN3 7PX UK
Telephone 44 (0)181 805 9088
Fax 44 (0)181 805 2440

Lestek Manufacturing Inc. (USA)
Brute high output alternators
6542 Baker Blvd, Fort Worth Tx
76118 USA
Fax 1 817 284 2153

Lugger/Northern Lights (USA)
Northern Light generating sets
Telephone 1 206 789 3880
Fax 1 206 782 5455
Netherlands Telephone
31(0)10 44 67 400

Mastervolt UK
Hart Inverters, battery monitors, electrical panels
Unit D5, Premier Centre, Abbey
Park Industrial Estate
Romsey, Hampshire SO5 19AQ
UK
Telephone 44 (0)1794 516 443
Fax 44 (0) 11794 516 453

Marinetics Inc (USA)
Electrical panels
PO Box 2676 Newport Beach
Ca 92663 USA
Telephone 1 714 646 8889
Fax 1 714 642 8627

Merlin Equipment (UK)
E-Meter/Heart Link 10
Unit 1 Hithercroft Court,
Lupton Road, Wallingford,
Oxfordshire OX10 9BT UK
Fax 44 (0) 1491 824466

Rolls Battery Engineering (USA)
Heavy duty deep cycle batteries
8 Proctor St, Salem
MA 01970 USA
Telephone 1 508 745 3333

Trojan Battery Co (UK)
Heavy duty deep cycle batteries
12380 Clark St, Santa Fe Springs
Ca 90670 USA
Fax 1 714 521 8215

SAFETY/RESCUE EQUIPMENT

ACR (USA)
Person overboard and rescue equipment
5757 Ravenswood Rd, Ft
Lauderdale
Fla 33312 USA
Telephone 1 954 981 3333

Ambassador Marine Ltd (UK)
The Stripper – shaft rope cutters
252 Hursley, Winchester
Hants SO21 2JJ UK
Telephone 44 (0)1962 775405
Fax 44 (0)1962 775 250

Float-Pac Pty Ltd (Australia)
Air bags
Unit 4/31 Wentworth St,
Greenacre
NSW 2190 Australia
Fax: 61 2 742 5565

Forespar (USA)
Lightning Master and other marine products
22322 Gilberto, Rancho Santa
Margarita Ca 926 88 USA
Telephone 1 714 858 8820
Fax 1 714 858 0505

Morglasco Ltd (UK)
Person overboard recovery slings
Bosboa, Mount George Rd,
Penelewey, Feock, Truro
Cornwall TR3 6QX UK
Telephone/Fax
44 (0)1872 870 139

Norseman Gibb Ltd (UK)
Ollerton Rd, Ordsall, Retford
Notts DN22 7TG UK
Telephone 44 (0) 1777 706 465
Fax 44 (0) 1777 860 346
Email Compuserve 10723.2744

Ocean Safety (UK)
Lightweight liferafts
Centurion Industrial Park,
Bitterne Rd West,
Southampton SO18 1UB UK
Telephone 44 (0)1703 333 334
Fax 44 (0)1703 333 360

Porta-Bote (UK)
Folding dinghies
The Barn Snowdrop Cottage,
Winchester Rd, Kings Somborne,
Stockbridge, Hants
SO20 6NY UK
Tel/Fax 44 (0) 1794 388046

RFD Life rafts
The Mill, Berwick, Nr. Polgate,
East Sussex BN26 6SZ UK
Telephone 44 (0) 1323 870 092

Swiftlik (USA)
Affordable coastal life raft/rescue pod
1325E State St, Trenton
NJ 08609 USA
Telephone 1 609 587 3300
Fax 1 609 586 6647

MARINE PUMPS/WIND GENERATORS

Ericson Safety Pump Corporation, (USA)
Bilge pumps
435 Roosevelt Blvd., Tarpon
Springs, FL 34689 USA
Fax (813) 934 6890
International faxes
+1 813 934 6390.
LVM (UK)
Marine pumps and Aerogen wind generators
Aerogen House, Old Oak Close,
Arlesey,
Bedfordshire, SG15 6XD UK
Telephone 44 (0)1 462 733 336
Fax 44 (0)1 462 730 466

LVM Products(USA)
Marine pumps, Aerogen wind generators and a range of solar panels
125 Mixville Rd, Cheshire Ct,
06410 USA
Tel/Fax 1 203 272 7059

Rule Industries Inc (USA)
All types of marine pumps
Cape Ann Industrial Park
Gloucester MA 01930 USA
Telephone 1 508 281 0440

Speedseal (UK)
Safety water pump impeller cover
30A Marrylands Rd, Bookham
KT23 2HW UK
Tel/Fax
44 (0)1372 451 992

Whale (USA)
Whale bilge (manual) and galley pumps
30 Barnet Blv, New Bedford,
MA 012745 USA
Telephone 1 508 995 7000
Fax 1 508 998 5359

MISCELLANEOUS EQUIPMENT

Dickinson Stoves (Canada)
Diesel powered galley and heating stoves
407 – 204 Cayer St, Coquitlam
BC V3K 5B1 Canada
Telephone 1 605 525 6444

M G Duff Marine Ltd
Zinc and Magnesium anodes
Unit 2 West, 68 Bognor Rd,
Chichester. West Sussex
PO19 2NS UK
Telephone +44 (0) 1234 533 336
Fax +44 (0) 1234 533422

Norseman Marine USA Inc
(USA)
Masts and Rigging, Norseman fittings (USA)
516 West Las Olas Blvd., Fort Lauderdale
Florida 33312 USA
Telephone 1 954 467 1407
Fax 1 954 462 3470

Scanmar International
Self-steering windvanes
432 South 1st St, Richmond
CA 94804 USA
Telephone 1 510 215 2010
Fax 1 510 215 5005

Village Marine Tech. (USA)
Watermakers
2000 West 135th St, Gardenia
Ca 90249 USA
Fax 1 310 5383048

MAPS/GUIDES

CBL Editions (France)
French waterway guide maps (recommended)
BP 21, 11401 Castlenaudary,
Cedex, France
Telephone 33 68 231751
Fax 33 68 233 392

Voies Navigables de France
(France)
French canal information, vignettes, Vagnon Carte de Plaisance
175 Rue Ludovic, Boutieux BP 820,62408
Bethune Cedex France

Shepparton Swan (UK)
Canal cruising guides and books
The Clock House, Upper Harliford, Shepparton,
Middlesex TW17 8RU UK
Telephone 44 (0)1932 783319

HELPFUL ORGANISATIONS

Cruising Association (UK)
CA House
1 Northey Street,
Limehouse Basin
London E14 8BT UK
Telephone 44 (0) 171 537 2828

Registrar of British Ships (UK)
SSR Registrar
PO Box 165 Cardiff
CF4 5FU UK
Telephone 44 (0) 1222 747333

The Royal Yachting Association
(UK)
RYA House, Romsey Rd,
Eastleigh
Hants SO5O 9YA UK
Telephone 44 (0) 1703 629 962
& 44 (0) 1703 627 400
Fax 44 (0) 1703 629 924

Boatline (UK)
Meadlake Place
Thorpe Lea Road
Egham, Surrey
TW20 8HE UK
Telephone 44 (0) 784 472222
Fax 44 (0) 784 439678

Boatline is a free boating information service run by the British Marine Industries Federation

Index